Limiting Power

The Case for Term Limits on the U.S. Supreme Court

Jack Thornton

Table of Contents

Introduction

Did you know that for almost 150 years, the U.S. Supreme Court didn't even have its own courthouse? Instead, its justices held sessions in spaces that were, at best, makeshift solutions to accommodate their work. It wasn't until 1935 that the Supreme Court finally settled into its own iconic building, where it continues to shape the American legal landscape today (*10 Fascinating Facts...*, n.d.).

Some think that the Court has always been an institution meant to be completely immune to politicization, a neutral arbiter of justice. Well, if you thought that, you're wrong, too. Consider the fact that John Rutledge, the second Chief Justice of the Supreme Court, served for just a few months before being removed due to his publicly critical stance against Congress (*10 Fascinating Facts...*, n.d.).

These historical quirks highlight an essential, often overlooked reality—far from being a pristine, apolitical body, the Supreme Court has been deeply entangled in the nation's sometimes messy political dynamics since its inception.

From the institution's earliest days, Supreme Court justices have navigated pressures and expectations shaped as much by political alliances as by the law itself. The independence of the Court, often assumed to be its defining trait, was never an absolute principle. In fact, its evolution reflects a jaw-droppingly complex relationship between law and politics that has only become more complicated over the years.

Looking back through the history of the court, there have been many instances where Supreme Court justices held ambitions beyond the bench; some even pursued elective office or advised presidents (Zeitz, 2022).

John McLean, a Supreme Court justice in the 1800s, was known for maintaining an active bid for the presidency throughout his tenure, while Abe Fortas, a 20th-century justice, frequently counseled President Lyndon B. Johnson from the Court's chambers, helping him draft speeches and policy statements (Zeitz, 2022).

This type of blurring of lines between politics and judicial duty was not unusual—in fact, at the time, it was considered the norm. At countless times throughout history, justices moved fluidly between legislative, executive, and judicial roles, often acting as close political allies to the presidents who appointed them (Zeitz, 2022).

While today's Court largely consists of career jurists and scholars, this close proximity to politics has left a lasting impression. The idea of the Court as being some kind of politically neutral institution is more modern aspiration than historical reality.

These historical facts reveal a challenging truth: The Supreme Court's influence, like that of any institution, has never been insulated from the political currents and social trends that have shaped the nation.

Growing up as a kid who witnessed the tail-end of the Civil Rights era, I was fascinated by the structure of American government—the checks, balances, and institutions designed to keep democracy in motion. Over the years, that fascination grew into a deep commitment to understanding and addressing the ways our system can—and sometimes does—fail us.

My career has taken me through the hallowed halls of law and public policy, where I've encountered firsthand the challenges and complexities of ensuring that government serves the people it represents.

I've witnessed the impact of judicial decisions on individuals and communities, and I've seen how a single ruling can hold deep ramifications that stretch out for multiple generations. These observations solidified my belief in the importance of a judicial system that evolves with society and remains accountable to the people it serves.

One of the pressing issues facing our democracy today is the lifetime appointment system for Supreme Court justices—a model that, while well-intentioned by the framers of the Constitution, now feels increasingly out of step with the needs of a modern democracy. Justices today can serve 30 or even 40 years, wielding tremendous power over social, economic, and political life.

This longevity, while valuable in preserving judicial independence, also poses risks. Lifetime appointments mean that justices are shielded from public accountability for extended periods, which can lead to a sense of detachment from the people their decisions impact (Navarro, 2023).

Instituting term limits for justices, as proposed by several legal scholars from both sides of the political spectrum, would preserve judicial independence while ensuring that the Court remains connected to the shifting values and needs of the nation (Wood, 2024).

The idea of term limits for the Supreme Court isn't new, nor is it without its detractors. Some argue that limiting justices' terms could expose them to greater political pressures, undermining their ability to make impartial decisions. Others believe that term limits might destabilize the Court by introducing too much turnover.

These concerns are in many ways valid, but I and many others believe that they overlook the benefits of a system where new perspectives and voices can contribute to the Court's work. In my opinion, an 18-year term limit, as outlined and endorsed by leading judicial experts (Wood, 2024), strikes the perfect balance. It's long enough to allow justices to build a body of work and expertise, but it also ensures regular opportunities for the Court to welcome new minds and ideas.

But beyond the legal and structural arguments, this issue is deeply personal for many Americans. Over the years, I've listened to countless takes from people across the country, from those who feel that lifetime appointments have insulated the Court from accountability to those who believe it has become too powerful, shaping the country in ways that no one could have foreseen.

Some worry that the current structure of the Court allows justices to impose personal ideologies on the nation for decades, while others express frustration with the polarized nature of judicial appointments, which often reflect the political leanings of the president who appoints them, rather than the will of the broader public.

In the chapters that follow, we'll take a look at how Supreme Court term limits could impact not only the Court but also the lives of every American. These reforms hold the potential to lower the political temperature around confirmations, reduce the Court's role as a partisan flashpoint, and ensure that no single ideology dominates the judicial landscape for generations.

For any American citizen invested in social and constitutional issues—from civil rights to healthcare to voting laws—the stakes are high. Term limits offer us a path to a Supreme Court that remains fair, balanced, and ultimately representative of the diverse society it serves.

In my public advocacy work, one of the most common questions I get about term limits is this: *How would limiting the time justices serve on the Supreme Court actually make a difference in people's everyday lives?* It's a fair question.

For many Americans, the Supreme Court can feel like a distant, almost untouchable institution, issuing rulings on issues we hear about in the news but might not see the effects of immediately. What they don't realize is that the structure of this institution, and its constitutional mandate, which enables life-long tenures, affects nearly every corner of American life—from the laws that govern our health and safety to those shaping our social freedoms.

Imagine, for instance, that each president had the right to appoint two Justices during each term, with each justice serving a single 18-year term in which they'd rotate between the Supreme Court and other federal circuits. Such a system would introduce a predictable and regular opportunity for turnover, potentially reducing the intense partisanship surrounding nominations.

Instead of waiting for a justice to strategically retire when their preferred party is in power—a tactic both sides of the aisle have engaged in—a term-limited system would ensure that the bench is periodically refreshed. One activist I've volunteered with has characterized these changes as representing a "clearing of the air," the idea being that if people know that change is on the horizon, it could relieve some of the political tension that currently surrounds every Supreme Court vacancy.

On the other hand, some more conservative thinkers worry that term limits might make the Court even more political. They see value in life tenure, where justices, theoretically, aren't beholden to the interests of the president who appointed them. But here's the thing: Lifetime appointments haven't been successful in insulating the Court from partisanship.

Today, justices tend to make rulings along lines that reflect the ideologies of the presidents who nominated them. And while they're not up for re-election, there's still considerable incentive to align with the political faction that enabled their rise.

At the end of the day, this discussion isn't just theoretical. Each decision made by the Supreme Court affects our society's laws, freedoms, and rights. The opportunity to reimagine how we appoint and retain justices could help restore trust in the institution by making it both more reflective of—and responsive to—the people it serves.

If term limits could lessen the divide, reduce the politicization of appointments, and make our Court more in tune with society's needs, then it's clear that this discussion isn't just timely, but is in fact necessary.

A Broken America

We live in a time when nearly every American with internet access can consume, share, and even create news. The ease of posting to platforms like TikTok, X (formerly Twitter), and Facebook has democratized information-sharing but at a cost: Misinformation is now widespread, transforming our collective understanding of truth and fact.

Studies have shown that fake news circulates up to 10 times faster than verified information, partly because social media algorithms favor sensational and emotionally charged content over balanced reporting (Micich, 2024). Misinformation today has the power to mislead and threatens to fundamentally reshape our perception of reality.

Social media platforms have become hotspots for mis- and disinformation, feeding conspiracy theories and distorted news to millions around the world. The effects of fake news and information go beyond misunderstandings; they can alter public sentiment and sow deep distrust. When misleading stories and conspiracy theories become ubiquitous, they begin to shape the way we view major institutions, from the media to the justice system.

Since the engagement algorithms of big tech companies prioritize the most sensationalistic news stories, many people may encounter only news that reinforces their beliefs or stokes their fears, creating echo chambers that harden societal divides. Today, with Americans increasingly relying on social media for news, the spread of false information is challenging our democracy, leaving us more polarized and less informed than ever.

Election Interference

No matter what side of the political divide you find yourself on, foreign interference in the US represents a looming threat.

At the time of the writing of this book, officials are sending out warnings that Russia, Iran, and China are engaged in a sophisticated, multi-pronged attempt to influence American politics. According to the Department of Justice, these nations have exploited social media and other channels to amplify divisive issues, hoping to sway public opinion or sow confusion (Klaidman et al., 2024).

The tactics used by these foreign actors are unprecedented in their sophistication. Russia, in particular, has learned to launder its messages through American social media influencers, enabling propaganda to appear homegrown. The Justice Department has cracked down on Russian misinformation campaigns, even seizing domains designed to look like credible news outlets (Klaidman et al., 2024).

While this vigilance is crucial, the sheer scope of the interference reflects a stark reality: The U.S.'s nation-state adversaries see our election process as a strategic opportunity.

The Rise of Authoritarianism Worldwide

In recent years, the global rise of authoritarianism has become a concerning trend, threatening democratic values and freedom worldwide.

As noted in a 2022 Freedom House report, autocratic governments are increasingly efficient in consolidating control by manipulating institutions traditionally designed to uphold democracy (Repucci & Slipowitz, 2022).

Authoritarian regimes use a blend of surveillance, legal reforms, and severe restrictions on civil liberties to undermine public dissent and maintain power. This trend is not limited to a particular region; from Asia to Latin America, more countries are adopting authoritarian practices, suppressing political opposition, restricting freedom of speech, and weakening judicial independence.

The impact of this global shift transcends international borders. International support for democracy has unfortunately waned, and authoritarian governments have started forming alliances, supporting each other economically and diplomatically, which further emboldens their anti-democratic measures.

In the current geopolitical climate, unchecked power becomes an international issue as authoritarian governments gain influence in global institutions, shaping international policies in their favor and limiting the global pushback against human rights violations.

This expansion of authoritarian rule underscores the fragility of democracy and the need for vigilance to protect democratic values on the domestic front. It stands as a reminder of the importance of active, informed citizens who understand the cost of freedom and the need to stand against governance that infringes on our individual rights and liberties.

Surging Corporate Interests

A marked increase in lobbying expenditures by corporate interests is yet another phenomenon that points to another growing threat to democratic principles today. As spending by major players reaches unprecedented levels (Reilly, 2024), a powerful imbalance is at play. Today, corporate interests increasingly dominate the policy-making landscape, often sidelining the needs and voices of ordinary citizens.

While lobbying is a long-accepted part of American politics, its current scale is further skewing American democracy into a system where only those with financial means can wield influence, skewing policy to serve private interests over the public good.

The implications of this trend are profound. When legislative priorities are shaped by corporate agendas, issues critical to voters—such as healthcare access, environmental protections, and economic fairness—can be overshadowed by policies favoring tax breaks, reduced regulations, or other concessions for large corporations.

In 2024 alone, the lobbying surge has been driven by upcoming expirations of key tax provisions, with lobbyists maneuvering to protect their clients' profits even as debt and deficit concerns loom large (Reilly, 2024).

This heightened lobbying also brings renewed pressure on lawmakers and members of the Judiciary to cater to these lobbying interests, especially as turnover in congressional staff has weakened historical knowledge of complex legislative issues.

Voter Disenfranchisement

The Electoral College, a system that has decided U.S. presidential outcomes for over 200 years (U.S. Election Assistance Commission, 2011), increasingly feels like an obstacle rather than an asset to many Americans, especially during election years with tight races. Recent polling conducted by the Pew Research Center shows that 63% of the population would prefer a direct popular vote over the current system (Kiley, 2024).

This sentiment has grown out of widespread frustration: Under the current system, a candidate can win the presidency without the majority of votes, as seen in both the 2000 and 2016 elections. This disconnect between popular will and electoral outcome leaves many feeling that their voices carry less weight, especially if they don't live in a swing state.

The Electoral College places undue emphasis on a handful of battleground states, creating a system where presidential campaigns strategically focus on select regions rather than addressing the concerns of the broader electorate. As a result, issues affecting people in non-battleground states often go unheard, reinforcing a sense of disenfranchisement.

Low Quality of Life and Decreased Life Expectancy

The U.S., once synonymous with the highest standards of living, health, and longevity, is currently grappling with a troubling decline in both quality of life and life expectancy.

Recent figures from The Social Progress Index attest to the severity of this downturn, placing the U.S. 28th globally behind much less wealthy nations such as Estonia and Greece (Saks, 2022). This decline, unique among world powers, signals a deeply troubling drop in social progress indicators, which include health, education, personal freedom, and inclusiveness.

Michael Green, CEO of the Social Progress Imperative, among other experts, has expressed deep concern over this issue. Green called the regression "remarkably bad" for a nation of such wealth and influence (Haynie, 2020).

Contributing to this downward trend is a pronounced gap in life expectancy based on income, education, and access to healthcare. Data shows that those on the lower end of the wage scale experience the brunt of these declines (Haynie, 2020).

The CDC reported that life expectancy in the U.S. peaked in 2014 and has since been undermined by a constellation of factors, including rising rates of firearm deaths, drug overdoses, and lifestyle-related diseases (Bailey, 2024).

A separate issue compounding this decline is access to healthcare. While the U.S. ranks fourth in medical technology, it places 97th in healthcare access (Saks, 2022), reflecting a massive disparity in who benefits from the country's world-class hospitals and breakthrough medical advancements.

Again here, lower-income households bear the brunt of this burden, as they're disproportionately impacted by healthcare costs and are thereby more likely to delay or avoid medical treatment (Saks, 2022). These realities clash sharply with the United States' self-image as a first-world country and reveal a society where quality of life and longevity are increasingly privileges of the affluent.

The disparity in quality of life and life expectancy in the U.S. speaks to a deeper, systemic issue that goes beyond individual behaviors. The country's status as a global outlier in declining social progress raises difficult questions about the sustainability of the American dream for the majority of its citizens, or whether well-being and a decent quality of life is now something only attainable by a select few.

Without urgent institutional and policy reforms, including reforms to the Supreme Court, the U.S. risks deepening the social divides that already threaten its democratic ideals in profound ways.

There's Still Hope, and There's Still Time to Act: The Time To Act is Now!

While it's clear that everyday Americans face a whole range of challenges, none of them are insurmountable obstacles. Yes, they threaten the very foundation of our democracy and test the resilience of our institutions. But there is hope: The power to change course lies with us, the people!

As American citizens, we possess a unique ability to protect, refine, and hold accountable the institutions designed to uphold democracy and balance power, with the Supreme Court being a central pillar among them.

In this book, we'll be looking at just that: the Supreme Court's crucial role in shaping our country, the ways it influences and is influenced by politics, and why reforms such as term limits are not only feasible but essential. But before we can explore these solutions, we need to understand the vision of the Founding Fathers—what they intended when creating the judiciary and legislative branches.

Only after we have a clear understanding of our constitutional foundations can we start to do the work to restore and strengthen the system in a way that aligns with the democratic values the country was founded upon.

Chapter 1:

A Very Brief History of The Supreme Court: Why Lifetime Appointments?

In 1789, the Judiciary Act laid the foundation for the U.S. Supreme Court, establishing it as the highest court for state and federal cases.

Positioned as a balance to the legislative and executive branches, the Court was designed to interpret federal law, maintain constitutional integrity, prevent government overreach, and preserve individual rights. Initially composed of six justices (*About the Supreme Court*, n.d.), the Court's structure and role have evolved with the country's changing needs.

The number of justices appointed to the Court has fluctuated throughout history, as political and societal conditions shaped its function (*About the Supreme Court*, n.d.). Today's Supreme Court, with nine justices, seeks to address the nation's most pressing legal and social issues, though according to a 2022 survey, 6 out of every 10 Americans believed that the Supreme Court justices were out of touch with the issues that mattered most to them (*Supreme Court Seen...*, 2022).

Modern debates around the Court's composition and influence, and particularly the practice of lifetime appointments, suggest the framers' decisions are worth revisiting. Today, as life expectancies have increased, Supreme Court justices hold office for decades (*Advances in Modern Medicine...*, 2018). The current system of lifetime tenures often extend a single appointment's impact across generations, usually turning each new appointment into a highly contentious political event.

Reflecting on the Court's origins, evolution, and present-day challenges reveals the need to consider new possibilities, ensuring it remains aligned with democratic principles and responsive to a rapidly reshaping America.

The Evolution of the U.S. Supreme Court

The role and influence of the Supreme Court have drastically changed since its founding. When it was first created, the Court was meant to play a fairly limited role—its responsibilities were mainly limited to the interpretation of federal laws without overstepping other branches of government. In my view, and in the eyes of many other reformers, this is what the writers of the Constitution had originally intended. What happened, though, was that over the years, the Court's authority expanded, and the institution took on greater power over a wider range of issues.

An important precedent for this broadening of the court's role and reach came in 1803 with the landmark case *Marbury v. Madison*. The case established the doctrine of judicial review. This meant that the Court had the right to declare acts of Congress unconstitutional. Chief Justice John Marshall emphasized in the decision that it was within the Court's power to have a final say when conflicts came about (*Judicial Review Landmark Cases*, 2014).

Throughout the 19th and early 20th centuries, the Court's role evolved as it presided over cases that would shape civil rights, federal authority, and the balance between states' rights and federal policies. Cases like *Dred Scott v. Sandford* and *Plessy v. Ferguson* exemplified the Court's role in contentious national issues (*Landmark Supreme Court Cases*, 2020). In these rulings, the Court regrettably helped reinforce racial segregation and ruled upon issues that denied civil rights to African Americans.

In the mid-20th century, however, the Court reversed course in a series of cases that reflected America's growing commitment to civil rights and equality under the law. In *Brown v. Board of Education,* which was ruled upon in 1954, the Court ruled racial segregation unconstitutional, overturning *Plessy* and marking a major victory for the Civil Rights Movement.

The decision fundamentally changed the legal landscape of the country while showing the Court's capacity to influence social change profoundly. This era established the Supreme Court as a key player in shaping societal values through interpretations of the Constitution (Debusmann Jr., n.d.).

Today, the Supreme Court's influence stretches across virtually every aspect of American life, especially when it comes to hot-button social issues like reproductive rights, healthcare, voting laws, and environmental regulation. The scope of cases that come before the Court attests to its ongoing entanglement in deeply polarizing political issues, leading many citizens to view it as a battleground for competing ideologies rather than a neutral arbiter of justice, a reality that's reflected in the surveys we looked at before.

Landmark decisions in recent years have also highlighted this shift, as the Court now operates under intense public scrutiny, with rulings that cut deeply through American society and garner substantial debate.

Why Lifetime Appointments?

The framers of the Constitution designed lifetime appointments for justices to separate the judiciary from other branches of government. This idea came from a long political-philosophical tradition.

When the Founding Fathers drafted the U.S. Constitution, they were heavily influenced by Enlightenment thinkers like Montesquieu and Locke. They chose to design the U.S. government with three separate branches—executive, legislative, and judicial—to balance power and prevent any single branch from dominating.

This system of checks and balances was intended to protect citizens' freedoms through limiting power in any given branch. The Founding Fathers believed that the government should serve the people's will while being restrained by the rule of law. Drawing from historical ideas of limited government and popular sovereignty, they aimed to create a lasting system that upheld citizens' rights and maintained a stable and fair society.

By mandating that justices serve "during good Behaviour," (*The Court as an Institution*, 2019) the Founding Fathers sought to remove justices from the political pressures that elected officials face, allowing them to focus solely on the law without concern for re-election or public opinion. This autonomy aimed to protect the integrity of judicial rulings, allowing decisions to be grounded in constitutional interpretation rather than shifting political climates or popular views.

The "good Behaviour" clause was intended to be a safeguard, protecting justices from retaliation by the executive or legislative branches and reinforcing the separation of powers. This security was especially pertinent in the early years of the United States, where the judiciary was still establishing its authority and legitimacy (*The Court as an Institution*, 2019).

According to a Harvard Medical School study, in 1789, the Supreme Court justices, on average, lived to be 67 years old. A little less than a century later, the average lifespan of justices had jumped to 82 years old. This meant that the length of a justice's time on the bench had increased from 16.2 years in 1850 to 26 years by 1999 (*Advances in Modern Medicine...*, 2018).

While this phenomenon allows justices to accrue substantial experience and expertise, it also brings challenges, as fewer appointments contribute to less frequent turnover and evolving representation on the bench. The extended duration of service not only impacts the judiciary's adaptability to new legal issues but also underscores the weight of presidential nominations, as each appointment has the potential to shape the Court—and, by extension, American society—for generations.

How the System Worked For Two Centuries

For much of American history, the Supreme Court's structure—lifetime appointments for justices—was both stable and effective. This frequent change in personnel seen in the early years of the Court provided a fresh infusion of perspectives that aligned more closely with evolving public sentiment.

In the 19th century, extended vacancies were common as well, often stretching over months or even years due to political conflicts or the slower pace of judicial nominations. In 1844, the seat left vacant by Justice Henry Baldwin remained unfilled for over two years amid political clashes between President John Tyler and the Senate, which at the time was under the control of the Whigs (DeSilver, 2016). Such prolonged vacancies were tolerated as an accepted part of the political process.

The system began to shift in the late 20th century as life expectancies rose, allowing justices to serve extended terms of 30 years or more. While earlier generations of justices might resign due to age or health, longer lifespans and modern medical care allowed justices to stay on the bench well into advanced age (*The Supreme Court Has Been Expanded...*, 2019).

This extended tenure has raised concerns about the concentration of influence in fewer hands and reduced opportunities for natural ideological change on the Court. It has also ramped up the stakes of each appointment, as a justice appointed in their 50s could potentially shape legal precedents for decades, well beyond the tenure of the appointing president.

This evolution in judicial tenure has led to discussions about reform, such as the introduction of term limits, to restore a balance more in line with the founders' intentions.

Does This System Still Work in Modern Times?

The concept of lifetime appointments to the Supreme Court has become increasingly controversial in recent decades due to its impact on the judicial and political landscapes.

While the original intent behind lifetime tenure was to ensure judicial independence and insulation from political pressure, the extended terms now common among justices have brought about some real challenges for the American populace.

Several current Supreme Court Justices were appointed at relatively young ages, potentially allowing them to influence U.S. law for up to 30 years. Justices Clarence Thomas and Amy Coney Barrett were both appointed in their early 40s and are likely to carry their term for over three decades. Justice Elena Kagan, appointed at age 50, is also on track for a similarly lengthy tenure.

Aside from the political implications of a slowing rotation of seats on the Supreme Court comes the challenge of a judiciary that's slower to make productive rulings on contemporary technology-based challenges like AI and automation, cyber warfare, and data privacy.

This disconnect was once mitigated by shorter judicial tenures and more frequent turnover, but today's long-serving justices may not understand the core issues around the ethics of advanced and emerging technologies. This misalignment can undermine the public's trust in the Court's role in translating the values enshrined in the Constitution.

Reform proposals, such as the staggered 18-year model mentioned earlier, offer potential solutions to these issues. By creating regular, predictable openings on the bench, staggered terms would reduce the intensity of confirmation battles and make the Court more responsive to changing public values without sacrificing judicial independence.

Lifetime appointments at one time served the Supreme Court well; however, modern shifts have revealed the glaring reality that these appointments may no longer be the best approach for the judicial system. Moving to a term-based system could help restore balance, uphold judicial independence, and provide us with a Court that's reflective of modern society.

Comparison Chart: Lifetime Appointments: Pros and Cons

Pros (For Lifetime Appointments)	Cons (Against Lifetime Appointments)
Maintenance of tradition: Adherence to a literal interpretation of the Founding Fathers' intentions.	**Low turnover and extended tenures:** With justices serving for multiple decades, there's a greater chance of stagnation and ineffectiveness.
Upholding of established legal precedents: Represents continuity in the court's authority and the precedent set by *Marbury v. Madison,* and subsequent precedents.	**Ideological entrenchment:** Longer terms may populate the court with ideological stalwarts who are subject to political influence and rule based on deeply- ingrained personal, and political ideologies and convictions.
Consolidation and continuance of institutional power: Lifetime appointments can be seen as a strategy for reinforcing the court's standing as an independent institution that's often, but not always (as seen during landmark civil rights cases) unswayed by changing social tides.	**An out-of-touch court:** Lifetime appointments may make it difficult for fair rulings to be made when it comes to today's pressing needs, especially where issues of technology are concerned. The concepts and ethical quandaries around new technologies may be difficult for older justices to grasp.
	Out-of-step with international standards: In other major democracies, high court judges typically serve fixed terms to maintain both independence and accountability.

Before We Move On

Now that we've taken a look at the Supreme Court's history and how the system of lifetime appointments came to be, it's clear that the system functioned effectively for much of American history, largely insulating the court from shifting political winds. However, increased life expectancies and modern political dynamics have magnified the long-term influence of each appointment, raising serious questions about the system's suitability today.

In the next chapter, "The Supreme Court Today," we'll dive into recent landmark cases that highlight the Court's role in addressing the pressing issues of our time—from reproductive rights and environmental regulations to voting rights and religious freedoms. These cases, including *FDA v. Alliance for Hippocratic Medicine* on abortion, *Glossip v. Oklahoma* on capital punishment, and *Students for Fair Admissions v. Harvard and UNC* on affirmative action, underscore just how much power the Court wields today, while also pointing to the deep divisions that sometimes characterize its rulings.

We'll also learn more about the current Supreme Court justices, whose diverse philosophies and decisions continue to shape the most controversial and consequential legal rulings in the United States.

Chapter 2:

The Supreme Court Today

As we've seen so far, the Supreme Court stands as a highly powerful force in American public life today, shaping the country's direction on a broad spectrum of critical issues from abortion and environmental regulation to capital punishment and religious freedom.

Each decision made by the nine justices currently on the bench has the potential to redefine rights, set precedents, and guide national policy for generations of American citizens. To better understand the impact the Court has had on Americans' freedoms, one only needs to look at the rulings it has made over the last few years. Through these decisions, the Court's influence is felt deeply, not just in abstract legal terms, but in the practical, day-to-day lives of citizens across the nation.

In recent years, rulings have touched nearly every sphere of public and private life, including some of society's most divisive debates. With justices appointed for life and coming from diverse legal and ideological backgrounds, the Court's interpretations of the Constitution continue to spark intense discussions over its role and responsibilities in modern America.

As the ideological divide on the bench has widened, each ruling reveals more about the justices' distinct legal philosophies and how these shape the Court's overall direction. By taking a look at recent landmark cases and learning about the perspectives of individual justices, we can gain greater insight into the nation's current social, political, and cultural landscape.

Recent Cases and Controversies

The 2023 and 2024 judicial sessions have proven to be landmark years for the U.S. Supreme Court, with decisions impacting a range of high-profile issues from reproductive rights to environmental regulations and affirmative action in education.

In this section, we'll review the most consequential cases from these sessions, taking a look at how each ruling reflects the Court's current priorities and the broader implications for everyday freedoms and rights in the US.

Abortion Rights: FDA v. Alliance for Hippocratic Medicine

FDA v. Alliance for Hippocratic Medicine stood out as a potentially precedent-shifting case in the ongoing national debate over reproductive rights.

The case questioned whether the FDA's approval of mifepristone, a widely used abortion pill, should remain valid after being challenged by a coalition of doctors. Mifepristone, used in nearly 50% of all abortions in the U.S. (Stening, 2024), became the focal point of intense scrutiny due to recent FDA actions expanding its accessibility.

In 2016 and 2021, the FDA approved measures allowing non-physicians to prescribe the drug and permitted the option of mail delivery, broadening access to the drug for patients across the country. The plaintiff, a group called the Alliance for Hippocratic Medicine, argued that this increased access to the drug jeopardized patient safety.

Far from being a politically neutral organization of concerned physicians, The Alliance for Hippocratic Medicine is in fact a front for a right-wing Christian group called Alliance Defending Freedom that openly opposes abortion solely on moral and religious grounds (Gira Grant, 2024).

While the doctors who participated in the trial claimed safety concerns, their claims were shown to be based on flawed science (Gira Grant, 2024). Legal efforts such as this can be seen as part of a broader strategy to limit or undo abortion access incrementally, following the 2022 *Dobbs* decision, which overturned 1973's *Roe v. Wade,* the ruling that had previously guaranteed abortion rights to all women in America.

Though the court ruled in June 2024 that the plaintiffs lacked standing, *FDA v. Alliance for Hippocratic Medicine* stands as a prime example of how politically driven legal strategies can use scientific or regulatory debates to influence policies on contentious issues like reproductive health.

Capital Punishment: Glossip v. Oklahoma

The Supreme Court case *Glossip v. Oklahoma* has brought up questions about due process and the reliability of evidence in death penalty cases.

Richard Glossip was convicted of planning a murder in Oklahoma but has maintained that he is innocent. His legal team has argued that important evidence was not provided and that legal errors affected the fairness of his trial.

A main issue, in this case, is whether the state's failure to share evidence violated Glossip's rights, as established by the *Brady v. Maryland* case, which requires the prosecution to share evidence that could help prove a defendant's innocence, and *Napue v. Illinois*, which states that a conviction based on false evidence violates due process.

The case raises an important question over whether multiple mistakes made in a death penalty case can lead to a new trial if these mistakes make the conviction untrustworthy (*Glossip v. Oklahoma*, 2024).

Environmental Justice: San Francisco v. Environmental Protection Agency (Clean Water Act)

In *San Francisco v. Environmental Protection Agency*, at the time of the writing of this book, the Supreme Court is currently reviewing whether the EPA's regulation on San Francisco's wastewater discharge complies with the Clean Water Act. The case will determine whether the EPA can enforce general water quality rules in permits given under the National Pollutant Discharge Elimination System (NPDES), even if specific limits for each type of discharge are not clearly stated.

The city of San Francisco has argued that the EPA's mandate is overly broad and imposes undue burdens without clear discharge thresholds, which could make it difficult for municipal treatment facilities to meet compliance standards. The EPA, however, maintains that such general prohibitions are essential to effectively regulate pollution and uphold the Clean Water Act's objectives of maintaining water quality, especially in complex ecosystems like the Pacific Ocean where varying pollutants may affect marine health.

The outcome of this case could significantly impact municipal water treatment protocols nationwide, particularly in balancing local operational needs with federal environmental standards. The Court's decision could redefine how the EPA enforces the Clean Water Act, influencing not only San Francisco's water management practices but also environmental regulatory approaches across the entire country (*City and County of San Francisco v. Environmental Protection Agency*, n.d.).

Affirmative Action: Students for Fair Admissions v. Harvard and UNC

In *Students for Fair Admissions v. Harvard and UNC*, the Supreme Court delivered a landmark ruling that fundamentally altered anti-discrimination measures in college admissions processes. In the ruling, the Court declared in a 6-3 decision that using ethnic background as a deciding factor in admissions at Harvard and UNC violated the Equal Protection Clause (Howe, 2023).

Chief Justice John Roberts underscored in his majority opinion, that any consideration of the ethnicity of applicants must be narrow and tied directly to the person's unique, individual experiences rather than broad assumptions based solely on race. This approach, he argued, reflects the Constitution's aim to eliminate government-imposed racial discrimination (Howe, 2023).

Justice Sonia Sotomayor dissented, asserting that the decision dismantled years of precedent and impeded progress toward racial equality, arguing that race-conscious policies had helped counteract systemic inequality and fostered diversity that benefits all students. Justice Ketanji Brown Jackson joined Sotomayor in dissenting, highlighting the lasting effects of historical racial discrimination and calling for policies that acknowledge and address these disparities.

The ruling set a precedent for most institutions of higher learning, requiring that initiatives aimed at increasing diversity must now avoid explicit reliance on race.

Discrimination and Religious Freedom: 303 Creative LLC v. Elenis

In *303 Creative LLC v. Elenis*, the Supreme Court decided in a 6-3 ruling (Bomboy, 2023) that the state of Colorado could not force a website designer, Lorie Smith, to create custom content celebrating same-sex marriages because it went against her stated religious beliefs.

Justice Neil Gorsuch authored the majority opinion, emphasizing that compelling Smith to express messages that contradicted her deeply held beliefs would infringe upon her First Amendment rights, particularly her freedom of speech. He argued that, because Smith's work involves custom expression, it constitutes "pure speech," ("Supreme Court Term October 2022...," 2023) which the state cannot lawfully compel in support of a message she does not endorse.

The decision ignited a major debate, highlighting the tension between anti-discrimination laws, which aim to prevent public accommodations from refusing service based on protected characteristics, and religious freedom protections.

Justice Sonia Sotomayor dissented, arguing that the ruling could undermine protections for marginalized groups in public markets by allowing businesses to refuse service under the guise of free speech rights.

Voting Rights and Gerrymandering: Moore v. Harper

In the 2023 case *Moore v. Harper*, the Supreme Court made a landmark decision that preserved the power of judicial oversight in the electoral process.

The question at hand was whether state legislatures held exclusive authority to manage federal elections without interference from state courts, grounded in an interpretation of the U.S. Constitution's Elections Clause. Legislators from the state of North Carolina contended that only they could determine the boundaries of congressional districts, free from judicial review under state law.

The Court, however, ruled 6-3 against this notion, with Chief Justice John Roberts authoring the majority opinion. Roberts emphasized that the clause in question did not grant unchecked power to state legislatures to oversee federal election procedures independently. Instead, he argued, judicial oversight remains essential to ensure that state legislatures adhere to both constitutional standards and state law requirements in redistricting and other election-related legislation.

This decision upheld a longstanding precedent allowing state courts to intervene when state legislatures engage in practices like partisan gerrymandering (re-districting), which could infringe upon citizens' voting rights. By affirming the authority of state courts to review legislative actions on redistricting, the Supreme Court reinforced the role of checks and balances in protecting democratic integrity (Bomboy, 2023; *Moore v. Harper*, 2023).

Trump v. Anderson

In *Trump v. Anderson*, the Supreme Court heard a constitutional question related to whether President Donald Trump could appear on ballots in the state of Colorado for the 2024 presidential election. The case arose when a group of voters petitioned a state court to prevent Trump's candidacy on the grounds that his actions related to the January 6th Capitol attack rendered him ineligible.

The Colorado Supreme Court ruled that Trump's conduct indeed qualified as engaging in an insurrection. The court found him ineligible to be on Colorado's ballot; however, Trump appealed to the U.S. Supreme Court, contending that this interpretation infringed on federal authority and could disenfranchise millions of voters by preemptively removing a candidate from the ballot.

In March 2024, the Supreme Court reversed the Colorado State Supreme Court's ruling. Chief Justice Roberts, writing for the majority, asserted that only Congress has the authority to invoke the so-called "insurrection clause" of the Fourteenth Amendment to the Constitution with respect to presidential candidates. The opinion emphasized that allowing individual states to make such determinations would create a "patchwork" of contradictory decisions, destabilizing national elections and potentially leading to voter confusion and inconsistent ballot access across states (*Major Supreme Court Cases from the 2023–24 Term*, 2024).

An Overview of the Current Justices and Their Most Notable Rulings and Opinions

Understanding the composition and viewpoints of today's United States Supreme Court is an important first step toward grasping the direction of American law and policy. The nine justices, each appointed for life, wield enormous influence over crucial issues like civil rights, healthcare, immigration, and constitutional freedoms.

Each justice brings unique perspectives shaped by their backgrounds, legal philosophies, and individual experiences, creating a Court dynamic that influences how laws are interpreted and applied.

As we saw in the previous section, in recent terms, the Court has tackled high-stakes cases on topics as diverse as affirmative action, women's right to choose, and freedom of speech, with rulings that reflect the complex interplay of ideology and judicial reasoning among the justices.

By exploring their backgrounds, political leanings, and most notable rulings, we can gain valuable insight into how each justice approaches their respective role on the bench, and how this collective body navigates today's most pressing legal challenges.

This understanding helps us, as concerned citizens contextualize current and future decisions, empowering us to better understand the evolving trajectory of American jurisprudence.

Chief Justice John Roberts

Chief Justice John Roberts, appointed in 2005 by President George W. Bush, is known for his moderate conservatism and his commitment to maintaining the Supreme Court's institutional legitimacy. His judicial philosophy is one that often emphasizes restraint and the importance of interpreting laws without venturing too much into policy-making.

Born in Buffalo, New York, Roberts excelled academically, eventually attending Harvard for both his undergraduate and law degrees. He clerked for prominent judges, including then-Associate Justice William H. Rehnquist, and built a strong reputation as an appellate lawyer before joining the Court.

While Roberts generally aligns with conservative principles, he occasionally bridges divides within the Court, striving to position the judiciary as an impartial arbiter rather than a partisan battleground.

Roberts's majority ruling in the landmark 2023 case we looked at previously—*Students for Fair Admissions v. Harvard and UNC*—stands as an example of the kind of measured, conservative approach he takes to the interpretation of legal precedents and the formulation of rulings.

Justice Clarence Thomas

Justice Clarence Thomas, appointed by President George H.W. Bush in 1991, is known for the conservative, originalist approach he takes to interpreting the Constitution.

Originalism emphasizes the original meaning of the Constitution at the time it was written over any subsequent interpretations. Over his tenure, Thomas has consistently favored decisions that limit federal power, protect individual gun rights, and oppose race-conscious policies despite being only the second African American to ever serve on the Court. Thomas's concurrence with Chief Justice Roberts on *Students for Fair Admissions v. Harvard and UNC* echoed this longstanding opposition to race-based policies.

Beyond his jurisprudence, Thomas has come under increased scrutiny regarding ethical issues. Reports have revealed that he received numerous undisclosed gifts, including luxury vacations, from billionaire and Republican party donor Harlan Crow (Kaplan et al., 2023).

These instances of potential corruption—often involving expensive travel on private jets and yacht cruises—have raised questions about the ethical standards guiding Supreme Court justices. Thomas defended his actions by stating that Crow is just a personal friend, and Crow has affirmed that they have never discussed pending cases together.

Nonetheless, these revelations have intensified calls for the establishment of a formal code of ethics for Supreme Court justices, as critics argue that such relationships can undermine public trust in the impartiality of the judiciary.

Justice Neil Gorsuch

Justice Neil Gorsuch, appointed by President Donald Trump in 2017, is known for his commitment to originalism and textualism, approaches that reflect his judicial philosophy of interpreting the Constitution and statutes according to their text and the historical meanings of their words.

Following in the footsteps of conservative stalwart Justice Antonin Scalia, whom he admired greatly, Gorsuch often emphasizes individual liberties in his rulings and opinions, especially those connected to free speech and religious expression. His jurisprudence reflects a broad interpretation of the First Amendment, consistently protecting religious freedoms and resisting state-imposed restrictions on religious practices.

Gorsuch's conservatism is balanced by a steadfast commitment to judicial independence, traits which often emerge in his rigorous analysis and precisely written opinions, both of which have earned him respect for clarity and intellectual rigor (Duignan, 2024).

In the 2023 discrimination case we looked at previously, *303 Creative LLC v. Elenis*, Gorsuch authored the majority opinion, asserting that the government cannot mandate individuals to express messages against their beliefs, framing this as a fundamental protection of free speech under the First Amendment.

303 Creative LLC v. Elenis underscored Gorsuch's commitment to defending religious and expressive freedoms against government intrusion, reinforcing his position as a key voice in the Court's current conservative majority.

Justice Sonia Sotomayor

Justice Sonia Sotomayor, a prominent liberal voice on the U.S. Supreme Court, has long been recognized for her impassioned advocacy for civil rights, equality, and protections for marginalized groups.

Appointed in 2009 by President Barack Obama, Sotomayor became the third woman and first Latina to ever serve on the Court (*Sonia Sotomayor*, n.d.).

In contrast to the originalist approach of Chief Justice Thomas, her rulings and dissents have emphasized the importance of the Constitution as a living document, with protections that should evolve to reflect the realities of modern society.

In *Students for Fair Admissions v. Harvard and UNC*, Sotomayor voiced strong opposition to the majority's ruling against race-conscious admissions policies, arguing that the decision would reverse decades of progress toward racial equality and entrench inequalities in higher education. Her dissent emphasized the vital role of race-conscious policies in providing fair opportunities and echoed her commitment to diversity and inclusion in both public and private institutions.

Sotomayor's judicial philosophy is one rooted in empathy and practical experience, aiming to ensure that the law is fair and makes sense given the dynamic nature of the issues at hand in America today.

Justice Ketanji Brown Jackson

Justice Ketanji Brown Jackson was appointed to the U.S. Supreme Court in 2022 by President Joseph Biden. Her historic appointment made her the first African American woman to serve as a Supreme Court justice.

Despite polarized confirmation hearings, Jackson received widespread support, including endorsements from conservative former judges. She was confirmed by a 53-47 Senate vote, even garnering support from some Republicans (Houck, 2022). Her personal and professional poise during the confirmation process solidified her image as a fair and empathetic figure.

Since her appointment, Justice Jackson has emphasized the importance of racial equality and social justice. Her dissent in the case we looked at previously, *Students for Fair Admissions v. Harvard and UNC*, alongside Justice Sonia Sotomayor, criticized the majority's decision to limit affirmative action, asserting that the ruling disregarded America's history of racial discrimination.

Like Justice Sotomayor, Justice Jackson's judicial philosophy is rooted in empathy and a keen understanding of social context combined with meticulous legal analysis. Her dissents and opinions reflect a belief that the law should serve all Americans, especially those historically disadvantaged.

Justice Brett Kavanaugh

Justice Brett Kavanaugh, appointed to the U.S. Supreme Court in 2018 by President Donald Trump, has demonstrated a conservative judicial approach throughout his tenure, particularly in cases involving executive power, gun rights, and administrative agency authority.

A graduate of Yale College and Yale Law School, Kavanaugh's early career included influential clerkships, notably for Justice Anthony Kennedy, whom he would eventually succeed on the bench.

Kavanaugh's confirmation process was one of the most contentious in recent history, marked by allegations of past sexual misconduct, which he vehemently denied. Following additional hearings and an FBI investigation, the Senate narrowly confirmed him in a 50-48 vote (Smentkowski & Houck, 2019), underscoring the deeply polarized nature of his appointment.

Though he is firmly a conservative, Kavanaugh has shown a willingness to align with the more moderate Chief Justice John Roberts in certain cases that emphasize judicial restraint, indicating a pragmatic side to his decision-making in cases where institutional integrity or precedent may be at stake.

Throughout his time on the bench, Kavanaugh's opinions reflect a deep-rooted commitment to conservative principles, especially in bolstering executive authority and limiting federal agencies. That said, his occasional alignment with Roberts signals a cautious balancing act, positioning himself as a voice that is sometimes willing to consider the Court's broader institutional role.

Justice Amy Coney Barrett

Justice Amy Coney Barrett, appointed by President Donald Trump in 2020, has swiftly become an assertive conservative presence on the Supreme Court. Her judicial philosophy, heavily influenced by her mentor Justice Antonin Scalia, adheres closely to originalism. This perspective is evident in Barrett's decisions and questioning style, which emphasize the textual clarity and historical context of constitutional provisions.

Since her Supreme Court confirmation, Barrett has been integral to several high-profile Supreme Court rulings, reinforcing conservative shifts on key issues. Her vote in *Dobbs v. Jackson Women's Health Organization* contributed to the historic decision overturning *Roe v. Wade*, signaling a new era for abortion regulation largely delegated to the states. Barrett's emphasis on state autonomy and judicial restraint in this context highlighted her commitment to limiting federal intervention in social issues, resonating with her originalist roots.

In cases addressing the scope of the government's regulatory authority, Barrett has frequently sided with the conservative bloc, alongside Kavanaugh and Thomas, advocating for narrower interpretations of federal agency power. Her approach has shown a preference for judicial restraint, particularly in limiting the reach of federal regulations that, in her view, may overstep constitutional boundaries.

Justice Barrett's presence on the Court has solidified a conservative majority that is reshaping the judicial landscape on critical issues. Through her rulings and incisive questioning, she has affirmed her commitment to a conservative judicial philosophy, impacting debates on religious liberty, executive power, and the limits of government regulation. Her originalist stance and rigorous approach are expected to shape the Court's direction for years to come.

Justice Elena Kagan

Justice Elena Kagan, appointed by President Barack Obama in 2010, has emerged as a moderate but influential voice on the Supreme Court, often seeking consensus in her decisions. Known for her pragmatism, Kagan frequently aims for middle-ground solutions, especially in cases concerning free speech and administrative law, reflecting her commitment to judicial restraint and balanced interpretation of the law.

She has been an outspoken critic of the Court's conservative direction on key issues like voting rights and environmental protections. In *Shelby County v. Holder* of 2013, for instance, Kagan dissented in the ruling that weakened the Voting Rights Act, arguing that the decision undermined essential protections against racial discrimination in elections.

Joining in the dissenting against *Students for Fair Admissions v. Harvard and UNC*, Kagan warned of the implications of the majority's ruling, underscoring her view that such decisions risk eroding hard-won progress in racial equality. Her dissent reflected her concern about the Court's increasingly conservative orientation on social issues and her commitment to inclusive interpretations of the Constitution.

While Kagan remains a firmly moderate voice committed to preserving democratic principles, her dissents in recent conservative-leaning rulings highlight her dedication to protecting individual rights and maintaining judicial checks on governmental power, marking her as a central figure in the Court's more left-leaning wing.

Justice Samuel Alito

Justice Samuel Alito, appointed by President George W. Bush, has served on the U.S. Supreme Court since the end of 2006.

His Supreme Court confirmation process was notably contentious, with opposition centered on his conservative track record. Democrats raised concerns about how his opinions could affect civil rights, women's rights, and limits on executive power.

His 58-42 confirmation vote largely followed party lines, with only four Democrats supporting his appointment and one Republican voting against him (Houk & Smenthkowski, 2024). Some Democratic senators attempted to filibuster the nomination, citing concerns over Alito's potential to push the Court further right. However, Republicans were able to secure the votes needed for cloture, allowing his nomination to proceed to a vote.

On the Supreme Court, Alito has been a consistent conservative voice, influencing major rulings on topics such as gun rights, free speech, and federal authority. He also played an active role in the deliberations for *Dobbs v. Jackson Women's Health Organization.*

More recently, his push for state authority over social media content moderation sparked internal division in the Court, ultimately leading to his loss of the majority opinion when Justices Barrett and Jackson shifted their support (Biskupic, 2024).

Alito's strict interpretive approach, combined with his extensive experience in federal roles, has solidified his reputation as a conservative stalwart on the bench.

Before We Move On

Now that we've learned a bit about each justice's legal career and the decisions they've made, we see a complex interplay emerge—one that's largely informed by personal political inclinations, judicial philosophies, and shifting dynamics in society that collude together to shape the highest court.

As we've seen, the Supreme Court is far from an isolated institution; it always operates within a broader societal and political context that has an outsized impact on its perceived neutrality and public trust.

As we turn to the next chapter, we'll continue our exploration by looking at the historical precedents that hinted at the political influences we witness within the Court today. Understanding these early signals is crucial for addressing and mitigating the politicization of judicial bodies that were originally designed to be impartial and independent. Through this close examination, we can start to uncover pathways toward reaffirming the non-political foundation of our most revered institutions.

Chapter 3:

How Judicial Institutions Can Become Politicized

The politicization of the U.S. Supreme Court is far from a new phenomenon. As noted in this book's introduction, from its very inception, the Court has navigated the complex currents of political influence and public expectation, often at odds with its intended role as an impartial arbiter of justice.

Marbury v. Madison set the precedent for the evolution of the Court by establishing the institution's authority over judicial review, enabling it to declare legislation unconstitutional if it conflicted with the foundational principles of the Constitution. This newfound authority elevated the Court's political standing, as it provided a powerful check against both Congress and the executive branch.

As the first judicial body with such a mandate, the Supreme Court's decisions inevitably began to carry weight in shaping national policy while also being subject to political currents.

American Judicial Authority and Early Political Dynamics

The foundations of the Supreme Court as a political entity were first laid with the Judiciary Act of 1789 which was ratified by Congress and signed into law by President George Washington. The act established a framework for the judicial branch, creating not only the Supreme Court but also lower district and circuit courts.

This legislation set the Court's initial structure, assigning six justices to interpret and uphold federal laws across the nation, thereby deeply ingraining the idea of judicial review into the American political process. With this structure in place, early justices began interpreting the Constitution in ways that would come to influence U.S. politics for decades.

The Court's size was altered multiple times, reflecting the political climate and strategic intentions of Congress during critical periods of U.S. history. From the initial six justices, the number of seats shifted several times, aligning with the number of federal judicial circuits to streamline the "circuit riding" responsibilities that required justices to travel and preside over cases across the circuits (*Supreme Court and Congress*, 2020). This strenuous task was intended to ensure that the justices were attuned to regional issues and state law during the Civil War. Congress expanded the Court to ten justices, a move that coincided with the establishment of a tenth judicial circuit.

In 1803, *Marbury v. Madison* made judicial review a core function of the Court, giving it even greater authority. Chief Justice John Marshall's declaration: "It is emphatically the province of the judicial department to say what the law is" (*The Court and Constitutional Interpretation*, 2023) cemented the Court's role in defining constitutional parameters, positioning it as an incredibly powerful voice in the nation's political structure.

Throughout the 19th century, the U.S. Congress wielded its authority over the structure of the Supreme Court as a political tool. However, in 1866, as the Reconstruction era began, Congress acted to reduce the Court's size to seven justices. This decision was primarily motivated by a desire to limit the influence of President Andrew Johnson, who was at odds with Congress over Reconstruction policies. By reducing the number of seats, Congress effectively barred Johnson from appointing justices who might oppose Reconstruction, ensuring that the Court would be more likely to uphold the newly established policies designed to reshape the South following the Civil War.

In 1869, a reversion to the nine-member Supreme Court was made by Congress under President Ulysses S. Grant's administration. The adjustment reflected a post-Reconstruction shift away from the size changes made during Johnson's presidency. The nine-member structure has since become the standard and has endured despite later efforts to alter it, most famously during the New Deal era when the court became a political battleground for influence over the nation's legal trajectory.

This Politicization of The U.S. Supreme Court

It wasn't until the 20th century that the Supreme Court became the focal point of political maneuvering we know it as today. This transformation is often traced back to President Franklin D. Roosevelt's tenure. As part of his efforts to enact the New Deal—a set of transformative economic and social programs designed to address the Great Depression—Roosevelt encountered substantial resistance from the Supreme Court.

The Court, with its conservative-leaning justices, repeatedly struck down key New Deal measures, viewing them as overreaches of federal authority. Frustrated by this judicial roadblock, Roosevelt proposed "court-packing" legislation, which aimed to add additional justices to the Supreme Court. He was ultimately unsuccessful in doing so.

Roosevelt's Court-Packing Plan

Roosevelt's proposal sought to appoint one new justice for each current justice over the age of seventy who refused to retire, with a maximum increase of six justices (Berman et al., 2023). If successful, the measure would have enabled Roosevelt to swiftly appoint a majority favorable to his policies. However, despite his strong political influence, Roosevelt's plan met with fierce opposition in Congress, particularly in the Senate Judiciary Committee, which viewed the proposal as an infringement on judicial independence and a dangerous expansion of executive power.

The Committee's report expressed deep concern that Roosevelt's initiative undermined the principle of judicial independence, a core tenet enshrined in Article III of the Constitution, which as noted previously ensures that justices hold office "during good Behaviour" (*The Court as an Institution*, 2019) and also stipulates that they receive stable compensation to insulate them from political pressures.

Ultimately, Roosevelt's court-packing attempt failed, as even his allies in Congress were unwilling to support a plan they saw as a potential threat to the integrity and balance of the judicial system. Notably, this early attempt at reform illustrated the extent to which the Court could become a battleground for ideological and political control, underscoring the ongoing tension between judicial independence and political influence and providing a model of how not to approach future reform efforts.

If we want future reform measures to succeed, they should not be so heavy-handed, should not compromise the Court's independence, and will absolutely need bipartisan support.

Ideological Entrenchment Sets In

While Roosevelt's emergency reform efforts were not successful, one important point they raised was that the long tenure of Supreme Court justices can contribute significantly to ideological polarization, often resulting in a Court that becomes rigid in its outlook over time.

Because justices serve lifetime appointments, they may remain on the bench for decades, far removed from the social, political, and cultural shifts that defined the period when they were first appointed.

Life tenure was intended to protect judicial independence by shielding justices from political pressures, enabling them to interpret the law based solely on their understanding of the Constitution. However, the physical challenges of the "riding circuit" system kept them closer to public opinion and regional contexts. Today, on the other hand, where circuit-riding requirements are a thing of the past, justices tend to serve much longer. Their prolonged influence amplifies the power of the era and ideology from which they were appointed, and in turn, this tends to lead to a Court that remains ideologically static even as the nation's political landscape evolves.

This modern reality, which the framers of the Constitution never could have anticipated, further entrenches ideological polarization within the Court and can reduce its connection to the evolving democratic views of the public.

Old Age and Mental Fitness Concerns

In recent decades, Supreme Court justices have frequently served into their 80s (*Life Tenure for Federal Judges...*, 2011), shaping critical rulings that impact American society. While life tenure was originally intended to promote judicial independence, modern healthcare advancements mean justices today can serve much longer than the founders anticipated and can even mean that their mental capacities decline before retirement.

Cognitive decline is an increasing concern for aging justices and judges who continue to make consequential rulings even as they face age-related issues. Studies have shown that memory and cognitive abilities often decline with age, with approximately 13% of Americans over 65 experiencing some form of cognitive impairment (*Life Tenure for Federal Judges..., Dementia*, 2011).

Justice William Douglas's mental decline during his 36-year tenure, which spanned from 1939-1975, was well-documented by the press and raised concerns among his fellow justices. Similar cases of justices serving while experiencing cognitive challenges include Justice Thurgood Marshall, who retired in 1991, and Chief Justice William Rehnquist, who passed away in 2005 without stepping down (Cooper et al., 2022).

Justice Marshall struggled with hearing loss, and as he got older, increasingly relied on his colleagues and occasionally confused details, such as which lawyer was representing which side during arguments. Justice Rehnquist, meanwhile, exhibited slowed speech and noticeable pauses, prompting other justices to complete his questions for him. It has been noted that law clerks often assumed additional responsibilities to support Justices Brennan, Marshall, and Blackmun as they dealt with their own health limitations (Cooper et al., 2022).

Today's lengthy terms filled by increasingly dementia-prone judges differ sharply from the early days of the Supreme Court, when the average tenure for the first ten justices was less than eight years, with three leaving the bench for other roles (Cooper et al., 2022).

Without a formal process to assess a justice's mental fitness, the Court remains vulnerable to the challenges that accompany advanced age, with some justices serving in their positions despite cognitive limitations that can easily impair decision-making. This can lead to rulings that feel disconnected from the prevailing values and priorities of a more modern, diverse, and rapidly evolving society.

The combination of life tenure and the extended service of Supreme Court justices raises serious questions over whether the Court can remain in step with public sentiment and the evolving needs of the American people. This structural challenge highlights the ongoing tension between maintaining judicial independence and ensuring that the Supreme Court reflects, rather than resists, the progression of societal values.

Lack of Accountability

Lifetime appointments for Supreme Court justices can create a significant accountability gap, as these positions were designed to shield justices from the sway of public opinion or political repercussions. However, in practice, this means that they're never answerable to the electorate for their decisions, regardless of shifts in public sentiment or evolving societal values.

A Monmouth University poll showed that many Americans view the Supreme Court as increasingly "out of touch," with nearly 60% reportedly feeling the values of the Supreme Court justices do not align with the values of the broader public (*Supreme Court Seen as out of Touch*, 2022).

Unlike elected officials and high court appointees in other countries, Supreme Court justices do not undergo performance reviews or reappointments. This system, though designed to protect judicial impartiality, has sparked debate over its effectiveness in a democracy where leaders are generally expected to remain in tune with the people they serve.

Other democratic systems, including those within the European Union, have introduced checks and balances to ensure judicial accountability while upholding judicial independence. For instance, in many European countries, there are councils specifically for assessing judges' performance during their terms (Albers, n.d.). This helps the judicial systems of these countries strike a balance between autonomy and accountability.

In the United States, however, no formal mechanisms exist for evaluating Supreme Court justices' performance, nor are there mandates for retirement based on age or mental capacity. This lack of oversight, combined with lifetime tenure, has led to calls for reform, with advocates suggesting that regular evaluations or term limits could help the Court remain aligned with contemporary legal interpretations and public values.

As Columbia Law School Professor Thomas W. Merrill put it: Term limits could "help usher out judges with mental decrepitude and loss of stamina" without undermining judicial independence (*Pros and Cons of Potential Term Limits...*, 2014).

The concept of such reforms is not without precedent, as other democratic countries have adopted measures to ensure both judicial efficiency and accountability while safeguarding the independent position of their courts.

Outdated Worldviews

The prolonged tenure of Supreme Court justices, aside from the potential for dementia and other cognitive issues, can easily lead to judicial decisions that reflect the values and worldviews of the past, sometimes causing friction with evolving societal standards.

Justices who serve for decades often retain the ideological perspectives prevalent at the time of their appointment and may be vastly out of alignment with contemporary public opinion. This disparity can lead to rulings that feel out of sync with current societal norms, as justices continue to make influential decisions based on interpretations shaped by older contexts.

This phenomenon is evident in historic cases like *Plessy v. Ferguson*, where the Supreme Court upheld racial segregation. The ruling reflected the racial attitudes of the late 19th Century, legitimizing systemic discrimination that endured until *Brown v. Board of Education* overturned it in 1954, marking a shift toward civil rights.

Brown in particular stands as a classic example of how entrenched judicial perspectives, resistant to change over decades, can lead to outcomes that later generations must overturn or rectify to reflect evolving societal values and ethical standards.

Nonpartisan thinktanks like the Center for American Progress agree with what the Monmouth poll revealed and have noted in reports that lifelong terms give justices substantial power over American life, compounding their impact as they interpret laws through lenses shaped by potentially outdated views (Buchanan, 2020).

Through cases like *Roe v. Wade* and recent deliberations on voting rights, the Court's decisions continue to draw public scrutiny, especially as societal values evolve. Critics argue that to maintain legitimacy and public trust, the Court must adapt by finding ways to ensure a more balanced reflection of modern perspectives within its ranks, suggesting reforms such as regularized appointments or term limits as potential solutions.

The Court as a Political Prize

In recent decades, the Supreme Court has evolved from a largely apolitical institution to a significant political prize, with each new appointment representing an opportunity to shift its ideological balance.

This shift is particularly pronounced given the increasingly contentious and partisan confirmation battles, which view each appointment as a way to either solidify or challenge prevailing legal interpretations on divisive issues such as reproductive rights, healthcare, and voting laws.

The confirmation hearings of Justices Kavanaugh and Coney Barrett during the first Trump administration exemplified this shift, reflecting both intense public scrutiny and deep partisan divides. Today's battles, and the ones that are sure to come during Trump's next term, are bound to be seen as more polarized, reflecting fundamental differences in judicial philosophy and legal interpretation.

The shift toward higher levels of politicization we witness today is fueled in part by the longevity of justices' terms and the high stakes associated with each nomination, as presidents now prioritize candidates whose judicial philosophies align with their administration's goals, often aiming to impact the Court's direction for decades. This tactic was notably employed in the 2020 appointment of Coney Barrett, where her conservative originalist approach was perceived as a means to bolster conservative legal positions on contentious social issues being debated at the time (Walsh, 2020).

This ideological loyalty has transformed the confirmation process into a battleground that mirrors broader political struggles in Washington. Consequently, each Supreme Court vacancy garners unprecedented attention from the media, advocacy groups, and the public. This type of deeply divided and high-stakes political climate we live in suggests that future confirmations are likely to remain divisive as parties vie for influence.

The Increasing Politicization of the Court Today

Over the past few decades, the Supreme Court has experienced a marked shift in how its justices are nominated and confirmed. The modern confirmation process increasingly focuses on a nominee's judicial philosophy and stance on key issues, resulting in a process that is not only lengthier but also marked by intense partisan scrutiny.

The use of ideological litmus tests has become a common practice, with candidates frequently assessed based on their positions on hot-button issues such as reproductive rights, healthcare, and gun laws. These tests aim to predict how a nominee may rule on pivotal cases, thus helping political factions in the Senate determine whether a candidate aligns with their values and policy objectives.

This greater emphasis on ideological alignment is particularly pronounced when the President's party differs from the Senate's majority, as each side seeks to appoint or block justices who may influence U.S. law in a manner consistent with their beliefs, recognizing that the current system of lifetime appointments further amplifies the stakes.

Each justice holds the power to shape the legal landscape for generations, heightening the importance of each nomination and transforming it into a prolonged political battle. If Coney Barrett's rapid confirmation in 2020 showed us anything about how politicized things have become, it's that today, both parties actively seek to leverage Senate procedures in an attempt to shape the Court's ideological composition.

Today's confirmation process has evolved into a form of political theater, with hearings serving not just to assess the nominee's qualifications but also as platforms for politicians to voice their political positions to their constituents and to try to swing things in their favor.

High-profile cases like *Roe* and its successor, *Dobbs v. Jackson Women's Health Organization*, have further fueled partisan tensions, as many members of the Senate now question nominees with an eye toward their anticipated rulings on divisive issues.

The combination of these ideological litmus tests, lifetime tenures, and an increasingly polarized Senate has made Supreme Court nominations one of the most contentious battlegrounds in American politics today.

Before We Move On

As we've seen, the modern Supreme Court has become a focal point of intense political strategy, with each nomination carrying the potential to impact American law and society for decades. The increased politicization of the Court, driven by lifetime appointments and heightened ideological scrutiny, shows just how high the stakes have become. While these dynamics are impactful in shaping the Court's decisions, as we've seen, they also affect public trust in the judiciary and the likelihood of the Court as an institution to be seen as a fair and impartial branch of government.

In the next chapter, we'll further broaden our perspective by looking at how the structure of the U.S. Supreme Court compares to those of other democratic legal systems. As noted previously, many nations employ mechanisms such as term limits or mandatory retirement ages for justices—practices aimed at maintaining judicial accountability, reducing ideological stagnation, and ensuring that courts can evolve alongside societal values. The next chapter's comparative look at these policies and measures will help us consider alternative models and their potential to promote a more dynamic, responsive judiciary.

Chapter 4:

How The Court Compares to Legal Institutions Worldwide

Legal systems across the world reflect a wide array of historical, political, and cultural influences that shape how each nation administers justice and interprets the law. While some systems prioritize codified statutes, others depend on case-based precedents, or even, in some cases, religious and customary law.

In democratic nations especially, judicial institutions tend to be rooted in either civil law, which traces back to Roman law and the Napoleonic Code, or common law, which originated in England and prioritizes judicial precedent. To understand how different countries have implemented reforms in their highest courts, it's useful to understand the core differences between these two legal systems.

As democratic societies around the world have evolved, in many cases, their judicial frameworks have evolved alongside them to better serve the needs of the people. Many countries now implement mechanisms like term limits or mandatory retirement ages for their highest court justices, allowing them to balance judicial independence with accountability. These systems encourage judicial systems that can adapt to contemporary values, ensuring that judicial decisions resonate with current societal needs and expectations.

In this chapter, we'll be looking at these diverse judicial structures and will be comparing them with the U.S. Supreme Court, where lifetime appointments stand in contrast to practices elsewhere. By understanding how other countries manage their courts, we gain insight into possible avenues for boosting accountability and alignment in the

U.S. judicial system, giving us the ability to put pressure on today's lawmakers to advocate for a judiciary that serves society effectively.

A Primer on the History of Global Law and Legal Systems

Legal systems worldwide have developed through centuries of historical and cultural evolution, each adapting to the specific needs and values of its society. Among the most prominent systems today are civil law and common law, which dominate the legal frameworks of numerous nations, shaping how they interpret and apply laws.

Civil Law: Roots in Roman Tradition

Civil law, sometimes referred to as Romano-Germanic law, originated in ancient Rome and later gained prominence through the *Corpus Juris Civilis*, or the Justinian Code, compiled under Emperor Justinian I in the 6th century. This foundational code aimed to provide a comprehensive, codified system that could address a wide range of legal issues.

Over time, civil law spread throughout continental Europe, influenced by Germanic, feudal, ecclesiastical, and customary law, and later became integral to legal systems in Latin America, much of Asia, and parts of Africa. The codification movement reached its apex with the Napoleonic Code in 1804, a unifying legal code that inspired similar systems across Europe and Latin America.

Civil law systems are structured around codified statutes, with judges applying the law based on these codes rather than on precedent. The role of the judge in civil law is more limited, with the judge primarily tasked with interpreting the law as outlined in written statutes. Legal scholars, rather than case law, play a significant role in guiding interpretations, and decisions are generally not binding in the way they are in common law systems.

This approach, rooted in legal positivism, emphasizes systematic and consistent applications of the law, often relying on scholarly commentary and interpretation to resolve ambiguous cases. This reliance on statutes rather than case law contrasts sharply with the common law system and remains a defining characteristic of civil law nations today.

Common Law: Evolving Through Precedent

In contrast, common law developed in England in the 12th century under King Henry II, whose itinerant judges traveled across the country, resolving disputes based on local customs and previous decisions.

The term "common" arose because the law was meant to apply universally across England rather than vary by locality. Over time, the principle of *stare decisis*, or adherence to precedent, became foundational, establishing a system where past judicial decisions informed the resolution of new cases.

In a common law system, case law and judicial precedent are as important, if not more so, than written statutes. When judges encounter legal questions, they first look to relevant case law to see if a similar issue has previously been decided.

In cases where no exact precedent exists, judges are to reason by analogy, looking at comparable cases to guide their decisions. The binding nature of judicial decisions is central to common law, creating a dynamic where the law evolves as new cases reinterpret or build upon existing precedents.

The common law system is prevalent in former British colonies, including the U.S., Canada, and Australia, and continues to influence legal reasoning and judicial independence in these nations, among others.

Hybrid Systems and Convergence

While civil and common law traditions are distinct, some countries, such as South Africa and Quebec, have adopted hybrid systems incorporating elements of both civil and common law.

Over time, many civil law jurisdictions have started to acknowledge precedents in certain cases, and some common law systems have codified aspects of the law that were once judge-made.

Globalization and the increasing prevalence of transnational legal issues have also facilitated the convergence between these two systems, especially in international courts, where procedures from both traditions are often blended.

Legal Systems In Today's Constitutional Democracies

The historical evolution of these two very different legal systems is indicative of the various ways societies strive to balance judicial independence with accountability. The flexibility of the common law system allows for adaptation to changing societal values, while the codification inherent in civil law systems aims for consistency and predictability.

Both approaches have informed how constitutional democracies worldwide have structured their judicial systems. In noting these various legal traditions, we gain insight into how foundational structures can impact the role and function of courts and how they have shaped and continue to inform judicial systems and judicial reform around the world.

Legal Traditions and Culture

While civil law and common law form the backbone of many of today's judicial systems, countries and cultures around the world incorporate other legal traditions that reflect specific cultural and historical contexts to varying extents.

These traditions include customary law, religious law, and transitional justice systems. Each of these frameworks brings unique perspectives on justice and presents us with a wider view of the full range of judicial structures worldwide.

Customary Law

Customary law is based on the traditions, customs, and norms of a community, passed down through generations, and is often adapted to changing local needs. This system operates in many countries alongside formal civil or common law systems, especially in regions where formal judicial institutions may be limited or less accessible.

This type of legal system is frequently administered through local councils or traditional courts rather than official state judiciary structures, allowing it to address local disputes in a culturally relevant manner. For example, in Zambia, local chiefs have the authority to administer customary law within their communities, often regulating land use and other local affairs based on historical practices (*Customary Law*, 2024).

Customary law often remains unwritten and flexible, adjusting to shifts in social norms over time. However, its integration into national law presents challenges, especially when it conflicts with national legislation or international human rights standards.

Some countries require that customary practices align with statutory laws, ensuring consistency and protecting fundamental rights. In places like the United States, tribal courts within Native American communities uphold customary law principles, reflecting a system where local customs coexist with state and federal law.

Religious Law

In many parts of the world, religious legal systems guide both personal religious conduct and legal processes to varying degrees. Islamic law, for instance, is rooted in the Qur'an and the Sunnah and is applied in various forms across many Islamic countries, either as the primary legal system or as a supplementary source for specific areas like family disputes or inheritance law.

In Jordan, for example, Bedouin tribal customs, which draw on Islamic principles, are recognized for resolving certain criminal and family disputes, often through traditional mediation practices (*Customary Law*, 2024).

Jewish law, or *Halachah*, influences family and personal status issues within Jewish communities, especially in Israel, where rabbinic courts have jurisdiction over certain religious and civil matters, including things like marriage and divorce.

Though no modern countries (excluding Vatican City) are governed by Christian laws, canon law is followed by numerous religious institutions. Catholic canon law is highly formalized and codified, dealing with various aspects of church doctrine, practices, and member conduct. Meanwhile, some Protestant denominations, such as Anglican, Presbyterian, Lutheran, Methodist, and Reformed churches, have developed their own bodies of ecclesiastical law that focus on issues such as church organization, worship, and ministerial conduct (Scroope, 2022a).

These varying sets of Christian legal codes and systems primarily focus on the governance of church affairs rather than civil law. While not widely regarded as having an effect on judicial systems worldwide, ideas from Christian canon law has undoubtedly influenced some of the common ethical and legal debates in numerous predominantly Christian countries across the world.

Transitional Justice Systems

Transitional justice systems are another important area of international law to consider. International courts and tribunals have been erected to address large-scale human rights abuses and facilitate societal healing.

In countries recovering from conflict, traditional legal mechanisms may be insufficient to provide justice, especially in cases where local judicial systems have been weakened or are distrusted due to past complicity in state violence. Transitional justice emphasizes a holistic approach to justice, blending criminal accountability with restorative practices aimed at reconciliation and social healing.

The principles of transitional justice initiatives often include mechanisms like truth commissions, reparations, and legal reforms, focusing on affirming the dignity of victims and preventing future abuses.

For example, after apartheid in South Africa, the Truth and Reconciliation Commission allowed for a restorative process that emphasized confession, forgiveness, and reparations over traditional punitive measures.

This approach has since influenced transitional justice practices worldwide, demonstrating the adaptability of justice systems in meeting the specific needs of societies transitioning from systemic conflict to peace and stability.

The United Nations

International efforts in transitional justice were heavily informed by the United Nations and landmark war crimes proceedings such as the Nuremberg Trials and the International Criminal Tribunal for the former Yugoslavia (ICTY).

Today, both the ICC (International Criminal Court) and the UN stand as transnational legal institutions that have been instrumental in formalizing frameworks for transitional justice, providing guidelines, resources, and legitimacy to such efforts around the world.

The Legal Systems of Constitutional Democracies Around The World

To understand the distinctive judicial systems within constitutional democracies, it's useful to first differentiate between the governance structures of monarchies, republics, and constitutional democracies, as each has shaped legal systems and judicial practices in unique ways.

Government Types

A monarchy is a governance system in which power is held by a monarch—usually a king, queen, or emperor—who inherits their position by birthright. In an absolute monarchy, the monarch wields extensive or even total authority, with limited checks on their decisions, including judicial decisions that tend to align directly with the monarch's rule.

By contrast, in a constitutional monarchy, the monarch's powers are formally limited by a constitution or legal framework. In such cases, the judiciary and other branches of government operate independently, most often with a high degree of autonomy and an explicit mandate to interpret and uphold the constitutional limitations on the monarch's powers.

Countries like the United Kingdom and Spain are examples of countries where constitutional monarchies blend the tradition of a monarchy with a modern parliamentary system and a judiciary that operates independently of the monarch's influence, which comes to take on a more symbolic role.

A republic is a form of governance without a hereditary ruler where the head of state is usually elected or appointed. Republics commonly feature elected leaders who serve limited terms and are held accountable through regular elections. The judiciary in a republic is typically empowered to function independently, with a mandate to interpret laws and uphold the Constitution.

Republics aim to distribute power across various government branches, including the judicial branch, to prevent any one entity from exercising unchecked authority. Judicial systems in republics often emphasize accountability, and judges may have term limits or undergo periodic reviews to align with democratic principles of representation and responsibility.

In a constitutional democracy, which is a broad term that can encompass both modern republics and constitutional monarchies, elements of democratic governance combine with a constitutional framework that defines and limits governmental powers. These governmental systems typically include both elected leaders and a judiciary, both dedicated to protecting citizens' rights, and ensuring that government actions remain within the boundaries of the country's constitution.

The Role of the Judiciary in Other Countries

Courts in constitutional democracies are most often given a mandate to interpret and enforce constitutional principles but also act as checks on executive and legislative actions.

Many countries around the world have long recognized the need for judicial term limits and mandatory retirement ages to maintain a balance between judicial independence and accountability. These measures help prevent the long-term concentration of power in individual judges and ensure that courts reflect evolving societal values over time.

Today, in fact, most democratic countries have chosen to adopt specific tenure regulations for their highest courts (*Judicial Tenure*, n.d.).

This guarantees that judicial perspectives are periodically refreshed and limits the potential for ideological entrenchment.

Below, you can see a comparative chart based on resources provided by Judiciaries Worldwide (*Judicial Tenure*, n.d.). Though not extensive by any means, it gives you a sense of just how common mandatory retirement ages and term limits are in judicial systems across the world.

Legal Systems Around the World Compared

Country	Judicial Structure	Tenure/Retirement Provisions	Benefits
United States	Supreme Court, Appellate, District Courts	Lifetime appointment with no mandatory retirement age (Article III judges)	Ensures judicial independence, but may result in prolonged ideological continuity.
Albania	Constitutional Court	9-year term limit	Limits potential ideological entrenchment, ensuring judicial alignment with current values.
Aruba	Joint Court	Lifetime appointment	Promotes judicial independence, particularly relevant in smaller judiciaries.

Australia	High Court	Mandatory retirement at age 70	Ensures periodic updates to judicial perspectives.
Austria	Constitutional Courts	Mandatory retirement at age 65	Balances judicial experience with generational renewal.
Barbados	Supreme Court	Mandatory retirement at age 65	Maintains experienced judiciary while allowing for regular refresh of perspectives.
Belgium	Constitutional Court	Mandatory retirement at age 70	Balances independence with refresh of perspectives over time.
Bolivia	Supreme Court	6-year term limit, non-renewable	Ensures regular refresh of judicial perspectives without prolonged tenures.

Brazil	Supreme Federal Court	Mandatory retirement at age 75	Allows for long judicial careers with scheduled transitions.
Canada	Supreme Court	Mandatory retirement at age 75	Encourages judicial independence while ensuring generational turnover.
Chile	Supreme Court	Mandatory retirement at age 75	Provides stability while allowing for regular renewal.
Colombia	Constitutional Court	8-year term limit	Provides continuity while preventing extended ideological influence.
Costa Rica	Supreme Court	Renewable 8-year terms	Balances continuity with accountability through renewable terms.
England	Supreme Court	Mandatory retirement at age 70	Ensures judicial adaptability to societal changes.

Ethiopia	Supreme Court	Mandatory retirement at age 60	Enables younger judicial perspectives.
France	Constitutional Court	9-year term limit	Maintains judicial neutrality and adaptability.
Georgia	Constitutional Court	10-year term limit	Enables judicial stability while limiting lifetime influence.
Germany	Constitutional Court	9-year term limit	Ensures regular judicial turnover and reduces the potential for any one individual to wield long-lasting influence.
Ghana	Supreme Court	Mandatory retirement at age 70	Ensures experienced judiciary with opportunities for renewal.
India	Supreme Court and High Court	Mandatory retirement at age 65 for Supreme Court justices; 62 for High Court judges	Provides a balance of experience with opportunities for new perspectives.

Jamaica	Supreme Court	Mandatory retirement at age 70	Provides a balance of judicial independence and generational change.
Japan	Supreme Court	Mandatory retirement at age 70; justices face retention elections every 10 years	Balances independence with public accountability.
Kenya	Supreme Court	Mandatory retirement at age 70	Ensures a continuous infusion of fresh perspectives.
Lebanon	Supreme Court	Mandatory retirement at age 68	Maintains judicial continuity with periodic changes.
Lithuania	Constitutional Court	9-year term limit	Prevents prolonged ideological entrenchment in the judiciary.
Mexico	Supreme Court	15-year term limit	Maintains judicial continuity while allowing scheduled renewal.

New Zealand	Supreme Court	Mandatory retirement at age 70; retired judges may be reappointed temporarily up to age 75	Provides continuity while addressing judicial shortages when needed.
Singapore	Supreme Court	Mandatory retirement at age 68	Ensures balance between experience and fresh perspectives.
South Africa	Constitutional Court	12-year term limit	Ensures balance between experience and new perspectives.
Switzerland	Federal Supreme Court	6-year term limit, renewable	Provides flexibility with regular opportunities for judicial renewal.

Term Limits Around the World In Action

As illustrated in the chart above, large Western European nations like Germany and France typically employ fixed terms for constitutional court judges. German constitutional court judges serve a single 12-year term, ensuring regular judicial turnover and reducing the potential for any one individual to wield long-lasting influence.

France's constitutional court, too, imposes tenure limits to maintain judicial neutrality and adaptability. These systems highlight how such tenure policies prevent any single judge from maintaining a prolonged influence, thereby promoting a dynamic and representative judiciary.

In other parts of the world, countries including Japan and Mexico have crafted extensive tenure regulations aimed at refreshing their judiciary. As shown in the comparative chart, Japanese Supreme Court justices face mandatory retirement at 70 and are subject to public retention elections every 10 years, which allows the electorate to directly participate in upholding judicial standards.

Meanwhile, other countries have taken steps to implement reforms that go even further than the existing limitations. Mexico, for instance, has taken recent steps toward shortening existing Supreme Court terms from 15 to 12 years (Romero & Mega, 2024). The proposal also includes a shift toward judicial elections for nearly all judges—a unique approach intended to counter corruption but also one that has raised concerns about maintaining judicial independence and safeguarding against external influences.

In particular, Mexico's proposed changes reflect a shift from appointment-based judicial selection to one that's more grounded in the popular vote. This measure, which includes a Tribunal for Judicial Discipline with authority over judicial conduct, aims to address systemic issues such as influence-peddling and nepotism.

These examples from all around the world show us how countries adapt judicial tenure policies to balance independence, accountability, and responsiveness, contrasting sharply with the outdated U.S. approach to lifetime appointments for Supreme Court justices.

Lessons Learned

Mandatory review mechanisms and retirement ages help the judiciary branch of numerous countries across the world remain responsive to contemporary social and legal shifts. They limit the risk of a judiciary that becomes stagnant or out of touch with public needs.

By maintaining a system of checks on judicial tenure, most democratic countries around the world have already agreed that judicial integrity and adaptability can be preserved without sacrificing the independence essential to a fair and impartial judiciary.

The approaches of these other nations show us how intentional term and retirement policies can help refresh judicial perspectives, prevent ideological stagnation, and align courts more closely with the public's evolving views, thereby upholding the judiciary's essential role in democratic governance.

Before We Move On

As we turn our focus to the next chapter, *Imagining A Better Future Through Term Limits: Looking At Viable Models*, get ready to look at some specific models and proposals for term limits that could provide a path forward.

Our upcoming discussion will examine how the U.S. judiciary might benefit from adopting similar principles, ensuring that its highest court continues to serve in a way that reflects the needs, values, and expectations of modern society.

Chapter 5:

Imagining A Better Future Through Term Limits: Looking at The Viable Models

As we saw in the previous chapter, term limits and mandatory retirement ages have been enacted across nearly every democratic nation in the world. The importance of judicial systems maintaining both stability and adaptability has become a priority, particularly for constitutional courts tasked with safeguarding fundamental rights and interpreting foundational laws.

In Europe, with its emphasis on civil law, there are extensive frameworks guided by the Council of Europe and the Venice Commission outlining how judicial tenure and structure influence the overall health and legitimacy of judicial institutions.

Most notably, the European model stresses the importance of judicial independence while addressing potential risks of ideological entrenchment through mechanisms like fixed terms, staggered appointments, and mandatory retirement ages. These measures create a structured yet flexible judicial landscape, where courts can evolve with society while protecting their essential impartiality (*The Composition of Constitutional Courts...*, 1997).

The European approach often includes term limits and retirement ages for judges, which encourages judicial accountability by introducing new perspectives over time without compromising the judiciary's core stability. Term limits, for example, encourage judicial refreshment in countries we already looked at in the previous chapter, like Germany and France.

Similarly, staggered appointments, seen in transnational judicial mechanisms like the European Court of Human Rights, allow for periodic judicial turnover, promoting consistency in judicial philosophy while accommodating gradual shifts in societal values.

In this chapter, we'll see how these viable, proven models and frameworks offer valuable insights for the United States, whereas we've seen that lifetime appointments have only intensified political stakes while raising big questions over judicial independence versus accountability.

By considering term limits of varying lengths, staggered terms, and mandatory retirement ages, and being open to a few different options, those of us who seek reform can begin to envision an adapted framework that could be applied to the U.S. Supreme Court—one that balances judicial impartiality with responsiveness to an evolving society, creating a more stable, effective, and trustworthy institution.

Fixed Term Limits

Imagine a U.S. Supreme Court that evolves with society, introducing fresh perspectives every few years rather than entrenching decades-old ideologies. Fixed term limits for justices could make this vision a reality.

12, 15, or 18-Year Term Limits

Instead of lifetime appointments, justices would serve a predetermined span—perhaps 12, 15, or 18 years—before passing the baton. This approach, already seen in courts around the world, could easily be incorporated into our judiciary.

In such a scheme, justices would continue to act independently but within a framework that balances stability and renewal. Term limits could bring a steady rhythm to the Court's work, allowing for a more consistent reflection of the issues that matter to citizens and helping the judiciary stay grounded in the more pressing issues of today, rather than being grounded in those of generations past.

Implementing either one of these different fixed-term limit models, no matter which one, could help reshape the U.S. Supreme Court into an institution that's more responsive and, ultimately, more effective.

The Clear Advantages

Fixed term limits for Supreme Court justices promise a number of advantages, both structural and ideological, that could streamline the responsiveness, balance, and integrity of the judiciary.

While much has been said about justices being out of touch, it's worth noting that in some ways, they're supposed to be. Justices, whether serving in common law or civil law systems, should generally stay neutral when it comes to political influence and favoring any particular partisan message.

Regularly refreshing the Court's composition aligns with the vision of many prominent liberal legal scholars, such as Israeli judge and philosopher Aharon Barak, who has argued that a judiciary should anchor itself in "ethical values of morality and justice" (Barak, 1998) rather than conforming uncritically to the social or political tides of any given moment. This sentiment undoubtedly would resonate with any conservative as well, hinting at the possibilities for an agreeance that goes beyond ideological binaries.

Implementing fixed term limits for U.S. Supreme Court justices would offer a host of benefits that many legal scholars and policy experts across the political spectrum believe could modernize and stabilize the Court's role within American democracy.

Furthermore, fixed terms would likely alleviate the political tension that has intensified in recent years around each Supreme Court appointment. If looked at from this angle, the answer seems obvious: Get the U.S. judicial in line with international standards by simply implementing term limits now.

A great danger in relying on such reforms is political fatigue. Professor of Law at New York University School of Law Daniel Hemel noted in an article published in the Journal of Economic Perspectives (Hemel, 2021) that the stakes of each appointment are escalated by the lifetime tenure system, given that a single appointment can shape the Court's ideological direction for decades. With fixed term limits, appointments would be more predictable, reducing the high-stakes nature of each confirmation process, shifting the burden off the American people and the Senators that represent them in lengthy, high-stakes confirmation proceedings.

Hemel argues that a predictable turnover would in fact reduce the sense of urgency that political parties feel to fill a vacancy with an ideologically aligned justice, thereby cooling off the partisan struggles that surround Court nominations. Under a term-limited system, each justice's influence, while still important, would be periodically refreshed, allowing the Court to remain an institution of impartiality rather than a battleground of political ideology.

Another benefit of fixed term limits would be that justices would be in a better position to focus on their core duties rather than being strategic about retirement timing. Current lifetime appointments may incentivize some justices to delay or time their retirements based on political calculations—a phenomenon that may undermine the Court's image of independence.

With predetermined end dates to terms, the focus shifts back to each justice's contributions during their term, making judicial service a temporary but impactful role and mitigating opportunities for any kind of politically motivated maneuvers.

As we've seen, according to leading legal scholars, fixed term limits offer a path toward a more adaptable, impartial, and accountable Supreme Court no matter what side of the political spectrum you're on.

They could reduce political friction around appointments, keep the Court's decisions more in sync with contemporary societal values, and restore public confidence in the judiciary.

While steep challenges remain in implementing such a shift, these potential benefits mark a promising future for the Supreme Court within a constitutional democracy that values both stability and progress.

The Inherent Challenges

While fixed-term limits offer numerous advantages, they come with several challenges and potential drawbacks. A primary concern among legal scholars and practitioners is the possibility of increased volatility in judicial doctrine.

Under the current life tenure system, the gradual turnover of justices allows legal precedent to evolve incrementally, contributing to the stability of the legal landscape.

In contrast, fixed-term limits could create a more fluid bench, potentially leading to frequent shifts in judicial interpretation and reversals of precedent, which could destabilize key areas of constitutional law and impact the consistency of legal rulings across the country.

Another risk term limits could bring, according to those critical of such models, is the potential for heightened politicization of the Court. Some argue that limiting justices' terms would transform each nomination into an even more high-stakes political battle, especially in times of divided government, intensifying the already polarized nature of the confirmation process. Most reformers, myself included, vehemently disagree; however, it remains important for us to be aware of the opposition and their points of view if we're going to get serious about enacting any kind of real change.

Anthony Marcum, a former resident fellow at the conservative think tank R Street is among those who have argued that while term limits are designed to reduce the politicization surrounding the Court, they may inadvertently increase it by making each justice's appointment a predictable point of partisan contention. Marcum notes that each new appointment would carry the same weight as the last, potentially amplifying ideological rifts within the Court (Marcum, 2018).

Another view commonly brought forward by court reform skeptics involves the possible erosion of judicial expertise. Justices who serve life terms accumulate a deep understanding of legal doctrine, court dynamics, and complex jurisprudential issues.

Term limits may in fact shorten justices' time on the bench, preventing them from developing the nuanced expertise required for handling intricate cases and diminishing the depth of judicial experience on the Court. This for instance is why I'm personally in favor of an 18-year term, as I see it as striking the right balance.

Proponents of life tenure have argued that maintaining a stable body of legal knowledge within the Court is crucial for continuity in legal interpretation and for producing high-quality rulings that draw upon decades of judicial wisdom. This is difficult to argue against, but that said—it must be balanced with the fact that all the indicators we've been looking at in this book flash the warning lights, telling us that reform is in fact needed.

Additionally, retirements and appointments present a deep concern for some skeptics or reform under a term-limited system. The risk, according to them, is that justices might time their retirements to align with favorable political climates, or that political actors could manipulate the timing of appointments to influence the ideological makeup of the Court. As we've seen through our in-depth look, this is something already present, and reforms likely would not increase the prevalence of this regrettable feature of our current system.

Recent reform proposals, such as President Joe Biden's proposed term limits, have been criticized, some noting that while term limits might reduce politically timed retirements, they might actually introduce new forms of strategic behavior, potentially undermining the perception of the Court's impartiality. Such strategic considerations, skeptics say, could compromise the judiciary's reputation for independence and further politicize the process of judicial appointments (Burke, 2024). I say nay, but again—it's important to know that these views are out there, because those of us committed to reform need to find ways to counter-argue these claims.

Despite all these challenges by skeptics, some of which have some validity, opposing voices such as Professor Tom Ginsburg have laid out powerful testimony before Congress, arguing the contrary. In his 2021 congressional testimony, Ginsburg noted that implementing term limits with a staggered rotation could in fact alleviate many of the same concerns skeptics raise. He suggested in the hearing that predictable intervals for judicial renewal would actually lower the stakes of each appointment, thereby reducing the temptation for partisan manipulation (Ginsburg, 2021).

In his view, and in the view of the many leading legal experts in favor of reforms, a structured approach like this could enhance the Court's legitimacy without sacrificing judicial independence or the quality of legal outcomes.

Staggered Terms

In the staggered terms model, such as the one Tom Ginsburg advocated for in his Congressional testimony, Supreme Court appointments would follow a structured schedule, bringing new justices to the bench at predictable intervals—typically every two years.

This approach departs drastically from the current system, where vacancies arise only through retirement or death, often resulting in the kind of unpredictable, often politically charged, appointment process we've witnessed in recent times. Instead, staggered terms would establish a regular rhythm of judicial turnover, adding transparency and reducing the intensity that surrounds individual nominations.

By ensuring that new appointments are made consistently, staggered terms address concerns over abrupt shifts in the Court's ideological balance. Rather than the high-stakes appointments that occasionally shape the Court for generations, each staggered appointment would incrementally contribute to its evolving composition, helping to maintain stability.

In a nod to those skeptical of reforming the appointment process in any way, this predictable structure would be specifically designed to help insulate the Court from sudden political tides, encouraging a more balanced, adaptive judiciary that reflects societal shifts over time without any abrupt disruptions.

The Potential Payoff

The potential benefits of staggered terms could be substantial, offering a pathway toward greater stability and a more balanced approach to judicial appointments. By introducing justices at regular intervals, staggered terms might help guarantee a steady flow of new perspectives on the Court, allowing it to adapt gradually to changing societal values without any drastic shifts in its ideological balance or partisan encroachment.

This type of system would enable the Court to reflect the evolving political and social climate in a way that keeps pace with change while avoiding the sharp turns that can come from multiple appointments within a single presidential term.

One of the most promising benefits of staggered terms would be their role in diffusing the intensity of individual Supreme Court appointments that leading experts on both sides of the matter are so worried about. Currently, the timing of vacancies can concentrate the power to shape the Court disproportionately in the hands of a single president, especially when multiple seats become vacant in a short span.

With staggered appointments, however, each president would have an equal and predictable opportunity to influence the Court's composition, likely reducing the partisan battles that often surround Supreme Court nominations. Instead of periodic nomination battles with high stakes, staggered terms would effectively normalize the process, hopefully bringing on a calmer, more deliberate approach to selecting justices.

This model would also decrease the chance of large-scale ideological shifts that can occur when several justices retire or pass away within a short time frame. By spacing appointments evenly, the staggered approach promotes continuity and safeguards against rapid swings in judicial philosophy that may destabilize the legal precedents that are so important to common law judicial systems.

Such consistency in interpretation and subsequent rulings could help increase the Court's legitimacy, as the public would hopefully come to perceive it as less susceptible to sudden political pressures or shifts in government. The incremental introduction of new justices would help maintain the Court's alignment with contemporary values and public trust over time, implementing a judiciary that evolves naturally, without the jarring effects of abrupt changes.

Staggered terms, far from being a radical idea, in fact, represent a great compromise because they would provide a structure that balances stability with adaptability, positioning the Supreme Court to serve as a steady, reflective institution within the broader democratic system.

Legislative Examples

One recent legislative proposal that garnered attention for its approach to staggered terms on the Supreme Court was the Supreme Court Term Limits and Regular Appointments Act of 2021 (H.R.5140), introduced by Representative Ro Khanna (Khanna, 2021).

The bill aimed to implement 18-year staggered terms for Supreme Court justices. Under the proposed measures, each president would have been guaranteed the opportunity to appoint at least two justices during a four-year term (Khanna, 2021), promoting regular turnover and reducing the high-stakes drama often associated with Supreme Court appointments.

Among other reforms, the bill's main provisions ensured that if any appointment would result in more than nine active justices, only the nine most junior justices would actually handle cases and controversies before the Court (Khanna, 2021).

Justices who had already served for 18 years would transition to a "Senior Justice" status, allowing them to perform other judicial duties under the Chief Justice (Khanna, 2021). This stepping-down of duties approach aimed to create an orderly rotation that would have refreshed the Court's composition without disrupting the continuity of legal expertise.

The bill was referred to the House Judiciary Committee and subsequently to a subcommittee; however, it failed to advance beyond these initial stages and ultimately expired in January 2023 with the close of the previous year's congressional session.

While the bill sparked meaningful discussion about term limits and staggered appointments as potential reforms for the U.S. Supreme Court, it failed to gain sufficient bipartisan support to move forward in Congress. The legislative process for Supreme Court reform remains a challenging path, given the strong constitutional, political, and ideological debates surrounding changes to the judiciary.

While it didn't end up getting passed, legislative examples like Khanna's Act paint a clear picture of how staggered term limits could work in practice, offering a structured and predictable method for judicial appointments that could reduce political conflict and safeguard the judiciary's intended impartiality.

Mandatory Retirement

Implementing a mandatory retirement age for Supreme Court justices, such as 70 or 75, is another common proposal that's been thrown around. As we saw in the previous chapter, these kinds of limits are already used to great success in many countries around the world.

In contrast to the stepping-down of duties proposed under H.R.5140, a firmer mandatory retirement age for Supreme Court Justices in the U.S. would establish a formal endpoint for judicial service, ensuring a regular influx of new perspectives on the bench. As with H.R.5140, such a policy would serve to balance the invaluable experience and wisdom of seasoned justices with the need for continuous generational change, keeping the judiciary aligned with evolving societal values.

Recent cases have further fueled the debate over whether such a system fosters optimal functioning. One prominent example is the tenure of Justice Ruth Bader Ginsburg, who, to the dismay of some, chose to remain on the Court until her passing at age 87.

Despite her enduring commitment and influence, and her widespread celebration as a cultural figure—being the first woman to become a U.S. Supreme Court Justice—Ginsburg's decision to stand her ground highlighted the dangers of the absence of a natural retirement mechanism. While she was widely celebrated as a pop-cultural feminist icon (a role cast upon her more than anything else), many argued that her decision not to retire left the Court's future composition vulnerable to the shifting tides of political opportunity.

Ruth Bader Ginsburg: A Case Example

Justice Ruth Bader Ginsburg's decision to remain on the U.S. Supreme Court until her passing in 2020 sparked a highly complex public conversation about judicial tenure and the potential benefits of a mandatory retirement age.

For many, her legacy as a pioneer in women's rights and equality made her a de-facto revered public figure, and for some, she became an icon for a certain brand of female empowerment. However, even among her supporters, there were many concerns around her decision, many criticizing her choice not to retire during President Obama's administration, a decision which inadvertently influenced the Court's ideological balance.

This concern gained particular momentum as the Court shifted significantly rightward with subsequent appointments by President Trump, reshaping the judicial landscape in ways that some argue undermined Ginsburg's own judicial achievements on the bench, particularly in areas like reproductive rights.

Opinions on this matter held by everyday American citizens reflect a range of perspectives. There was substantial disagreement even among feminists who generally recognized Ginsburg's importance but wished that she would have made the decision to hang up her cloak.

On forums like Reddit's *r/AskFeminists*, (*Should RBG Have Retired in 2013?*, 2022) many users expressed frustration, with one commenter asking if Ginsburg should have retired to allow a younger appointee to take her place and potentially safeguard liberal values.

Other voices in that same forum contended that it was unreasonable for the fate of American rights to hinge on the decision of a single aging justice, pointing instead to systemic flaws within the judicial and political systems.

Lawyer and Ruth Bader Ginsburg biographer Linda Hirshman suggested in an interview with a Politico journalist that Ginsburg may have become somewhat disconnected from the "zeitgeist" in her later years (Schaffer, 2022), failing to foresee the radicalism of her political opponents.

In public discourse, the debate over Ginsburg's retirement has also highlighted deeper issues of judicial independence, age-related considerations, and the strategic timing of retirements. While some saw her decision as a mark of dedication, others saw it as a reminder of the risks associated with lifetime appointments.

The case of RGB points to the complexities and potential consequences of judicial tenure decisions, further fueling the conversation on whether a mandatory retirement age might help prevent similar controversies in the future.

Before We Move On

Each of the models we've looked at seeks to balance the independence and impartiality of the judiciary with adaptability and accountability. As we've seen, fixed terms and staggered appointments offer pathways to a more responsive, consistent, and balanced Court, while mandatory retirement ages provide a natural, structured turnover that ensures a continuous influx of fresh perspectives.

As we move on to the next chapter, *Big Payoffs for Democracy*, we'll be considering how term limits for Supreme Court justices could bolster democratic integrity. This change has the potential to not only mitigate political polarization but also reinforce public trust in one of the most enduring institutions of the federal government.

By exploring how these judicial reforms might strengthen and sustain democracy, we'll gain insight into the far-reaching impacts that a more adaptable, responsive judiciary can have on the nation's democratic health and future stability.

Chapter 6:

Big Payoffs For Democracy

In this chapter, we'll be taking a deeper, analytical look at three key payoffs that term limits could offer American democracy.

The first payoff we'll be taking a closer look at is the reduction of political tension: Term limits would ease the pressure that currently surrounds each Supreme Court nomination by ensuring regular judicial turnover. This regularity could transform nominations from intense, high-stakes events into a more routine part of governance, making it easier for the Court to maintain its neutrality amid political division.

Secondly, term limits could bring a valuable renewal of judicial perspectives. As society, technology, and global concerns evolve, the Supreme Court must be prepared to interpret laws within this changing landscape. A Court that regularly rotates justices would be better equipped to address contemporary issues with fresh insights, ensuring that its decisions remain relevant to the challenges of modern America.

Finally, term limits could enhance judicial independence by reducing the long-term career pressures that accompany lifetime tenure. Without the lifelong influence of political or ideological leanings, justices could make decisions based more purely on legal principles and precedents. This environment would encourage rulings grounded in law rather than potential career implications, which can subtly shape decisions over a lifetime of service.

Through a closer look at each of these potential payoffs, we'll see how term limits could help build a judiciary that balances independence with adaptability, making it an institution that's more in line with the democratic ideals it was designed to protect. This vision for a term-limited Supreme Court offers a model for maintaining judicial impartiality while ushering in the change necessary to serve an evolving society.

Reducing Political Tension

Under the current system, each judicial vacancy is a high-stakes political contest, with both major parties vying to secure lasting ideological dominance. This pattern has intensified over recent years, transforming the nomination process into a highly contentious, polarizing affair.

This shift was notably seen in the nominations following Justice Scalia's death in 2016 and Justice Ginsburg's passing in 2020, where swift and partisan responses to these vacancies led to substantial public debate and fueled distrust.

President Trump's swift nomination of Amy Coney Barrett to replace Ginsburg right before the 2020 election—echoing previous controversies over the halted Merrick Garland nomination in 2016—showed again how each nomination is now perceived as a battle to shape the Court for decades to come.

This intensifying competition over judicial appointments erodes public confidence in the Court's impartiality and puts the judiciary in an uncomfortable and unnatural position as a proxy of political maneuvering and deal-making.

What Legal Scholars Say

Research from Associate Professor of Political Science Miles T. Armaly and Assistant Professor of Political Science Elizabeth A. Lane that appeared in the journal *American Politics Research* emphasizes that these politically charged vacancies in fact exert a direct impact on public perceptions of the Supreme Court's legitimacy (Armaly & Lane, 2022).

Their research suggests that the open politicking to fill a seat—especially when influenced by partisan motives, as seen in the contrasting treatment of Garland and Barrett—leads to a decrease in diffuse support for the judiciary, particularly among individuals who feel politically disadvantaged by these appointments.

The study further found that, while Republicans may remain supportive of the Court under favorable appointments, Democrats showed significant declines in support when faced with outcomes they viewed as partisan. This growing skepticism reflects how the Court's role is increasingly viewed through a partisan lens, contributing to the perception that judicial appointments are a strategic avenue for political gains rather than a process of ensuring fair and balanced governance.

Other leading scholars in the field, including Columbia Law's Thomas Merrill, have observed that drawn-out terms allow justices to maintain enduring influence, often beyond the political administrations that appointed them. This dynamic has, over time, amplified political battles over judicial confirmations, polarizing Congress and the broader public (*Pros and Cons of Potential Term Limits...*, 2014).

In this kind of political climate, the stakes surrounding Supreme Court nominations are now, unfortunately, as much about ideological preservation as they are about legal expertise. Each vacancy represents a critical moment to advance or protect a particular political agenda, placing enormous pressure on the confirmation process.

What The Mainstream Media Says

A recent BBC article noted that this trend has heightened the perception of the Court as an ideologically driven entity, detracting from its role as a nonpartisan arbiter of the law (Debusmann Jr., n.d.). The resultant erosion of the Court's perceived neutrality raises pressing questions about the institution's role in democracy and underscores the need to rethink lifetime appointments.

By potentially introducing term limits, the focus of each vacancy could shift from a battleground for ideological supremacy to a more stable and routine transition of judicial expertise. This change might help restore public trust in the Court's impartiality and refocus the judicial nomination process on legal qualification rather than political alignment.

This intensifying politicization of the Supreme Court noted by research scholars and media outlets underscores the urgent need for reforms aimed at depoliticizing the nomination process and restoring public trust in the judiciary's role as an impartial institution.

A Potential End To "Lock-Ins"

With a predictable turnover enabled by term limits, the need to "lock in" a particular ideological view would diminish, as the next vacancy would reliably follow within a set timeframe. According to Tom Ginsburg's congressional testimony, which we looked at briefly in the previous chapter, this structured rotation could lower the temperature around appointments, making them less of a battleground. In his testimony, he also highlighted that such an approach could align the Supreme Court more closely with how other nations maintain their highest courts: by ensuring justices are periodically refreshed, thereby preventing the courts from being politicized during a single, high-impact appointment (Ginsburg, 2021).

If justices served for defined, fixed terms, the expectation of a regular rotation would allow political actors to move beyond all-or-nothing nomination battles. Instead, appointments would become more routine, focusing less on the enduring impact of any single justice and more on the broader, balanced evolution of the Court's composition over time.

This consistent turnover would help to alleviate the intense political strife surrounding nominations, reducing the public perception of the Court as an extension of partisan power and helping restore faith in its impartiality.

Ending Polarizing, Drawn-Out Confirmation Processes Once and For All

An analysis by the nonpartisan think tank the Brookings Institution pointed out that the current system of lifetime appointments has encouraged increasingly bitter and polarizing confirmation battles.

Regular, predictable turnover would instead introduce a level of certainty, allowing both the public and political leaders to anticipate and prepare for new appointments within a structured framework (Eisen & Matsuki, 2022).

Consistent renewal of seats on the Supreme Court would encourage a more measured, less combative approach to confirmations, breaking the cycle of polarization that has come to characterize Supreme Court appointments.

By ensuring regular vacancies, term limits could transform the nomination process from a political flashpoint into a routine aspect of judicial maintenance, ultimately helping to restore the perception of the Court as an impartial institution, insulated from the pressures of shifting political climates.

Reform Would Bring a Much-Needed Refresh

The Brookings Institution has also noted in multiple reports that reforms to the Supreme Court's structure appointment processes and term limit could effectively bolster the Court's alignment with public sentiment and contribute to restoring trust in the judiciary as an institution that remains responsive, rather than fixated on the modes of thinking of the past (Eisen & Matsuki, 2022; Wheeler, 2020).

This approach could alleviate the risk of decisions that are disconnected from the current societal context, allowing the Court to handle emergent issues—from digital privacy concerns to evolving civil rights frameworks—with an understanding grounded in the present (Eisen & Matsuki, 2022; Wheeler, 2020).

Promoting Judicial Independence

Lifetime tenure, designed to protect justices from political pressure, can also create unintended risks, particularly when justices cultivate long-term relationships with wealthy donors or ideological allies.

Without a mechanism to cycle out justices periodically, relationships between justices and influential benefactors have the potential to create public skepticism about impartiality. The controversy over Justice Clarence Thomas's extensive association with billionaire Harlan Crow exemplifies these exact risks.

Over the years, Thomas has accepted numerous luxury trips and other undisclosed benefits from Crow, a prominent conservative donor. Such undisclosed perks have ranged from international trips on private jets to stays at exclusive resorts, a degree of hospitality unprecedented in modern Supreme Court history (Kaplan et al., 2023). The absence of transparency around these interactions has raised concerns about whether personal and ideological influences might subtly affect judicial decisions.

These associations underscore a critical point: Lifetime tenure allows these types of relationships and other corruptive influences to span decades, leaving justices potentially susceptible to ideological or financial interests that may erode public trust.

Federal law requires most public officials, including members of Congress, to disclose any kind of gifts above a certain threshold, yet Supreme Court justices, largely exempt from these regulations, are left to regulate themselves in many respects (Kaplan et al., 2023). Unlike other federal judges, Supreme Court justices face fewer restrictions, which raises concerns about accountability in cases where potential conflicts of interest arise.

In Mexico, the recent push for an elective system instead of appointments for judges that we discussed in Chapter 4 can be seen as a response to the potential dangers of allowing ideology to dominate judicial selection and a desire to weed out corruption. That said, in the case of Mexico's proposed reforms, some have voiced criticism over concerns that an electoral-based appointment process could align the judiciary too closely with the ruling party's ideology (Romero & Mega, 2024).

Despite the risks, no matter the country, implementing term limits could help curb corruption and ideological entanglements by diminishing the long-term influence that wealthy and ideological donors might exert over justices. Shorter, fixed terms would reduce the incentive to cultivate long-standing alliances, aligning judicial actions more closely with legal principles and public expectations of independence rather than partisan interests.

These types of approaches, whether electorally-based or appointment-based, could also lessen public perceptions of a judiciary entangled with financial or ideological interests, increasing the public's confidence in the Court's role as an impartial arbiter.

Before We Move On

By reducing the intense political stakes surrounding each appointment and reinforcing judicial independence, term limits offer a pathway toward a Supreme Court that is both impartial and responsive. Research from leading scholars has demonstrated that these changes would promote a healthier democratic process while increasing public trust in the judiciary as an institution dedicated to upholding justice rather than swaying with political winds.

The Court's impartiality and the public's confidence in it as a nonpartisan institution are foundational to its role in democracy. Term limits provide a measured, adaptable approach to preserving these values while allowing the Court to evolve with the times. Through the reforms explored in this chapter, the judiciary could move toward a model that balances stability with the flexibility needed to remain relevant in a fast-changing world, while weeding out potential corruption and influence-peddling.

While term limits present clear advantages, they also face challenges and criticisms that cannot be ignored. In the next chapter, we'll take a look at some common arguments against implementing term limits for Supreme Court justices, including concerns over constitutional changes, potential politicization, and the risks of undermining judicial independence. By better understanding and dissecting these opposing perspectives, we can more fully assess the viability of term limits as a means of judicial reform and weigh the potential benefits against the costs.

Chapter 7:

Addressing Opposition To Reforms

As the debate over term limits for Supreme Court justices gains traction, unfortunately, so too does the opposition. Many critics argue that lifetime appointments are essential for maintaining judicial independence, shielding justices from the pressures and influence of politics, and allowing them to make decisions based solely on legal principles. Opponents of term limits believe that only by remaining in office for life can justices stay insulated from shifting political currents and uphold the Court's impartiality.

Others express concern that implementing term limits could intensify political conflicts around the nomination process. They often worry that with more frequent appointments, the nomination process could become a revolving door for partisan disputes, further entrenching divisions in a political climate already strained by polarization.

Additionally, some argue that term limits could undermine the continuity and institutional memory of the Court, which benefits from justices who bring years of experience and accumulated knowledge to bear on complex legal questions. By staying on the bench for decades, lifetime appointees shape and reinforce precedents, contributing to a judiciary that evolves thoughtfully rather than abruptly.

In this chapter, we'll look at these common arguments and try to understand why these concerns hold weight while also examining how other democracies and legal systems address similar challenges. By analyzing these objections alongside international examples, we can start to consider how term limits might be able to preserve and improve the qualities essential to the Supreme Court's role in American democracy, putting us in a better position to counter-argue those who oppose reforms.

Many Believe That Lifetime Tenure Ensures Judicial Independence

One of the strongest arguments for lifetime appointments to the Supreme Court is that they help protect judicial independence.

The concept of judicial independence itself is contingent upon the idea that justices must be pristine and unaffected by any external pressures—whether political, social, or financial. This way, the idea at least is that they can rule solely based on the law and the Constitution. As noted previously, Article III, Section 1 of the Constitution, says that justices should "hold their offices during good Behaviour" (*U.S. Constitution - Article III*, 1787).

Alexander Hamilton, among others, interpreted this to mean that Supreme Court Justices were to have lifetime tenure. Hamilton argued that life terms were, in fact crucial, because they allowed justices to make decisions based on legal principles, without fearing the consequences of those decisions on their careers (Herr, 2023).

This unique arrangement has led many to view life tenure as essential for maintaining a judiciary that operates independently from the executive and legislative branches of government. Unlike elected officials, who may feel pressured to make popular decisions or cater to special interests, lifetime-appointed justices are (theoretically, if not in practice) insulated from these concerns.

Unlike politicians, Supreme Court Justices don't need to worry about re-election, campaign donors, or appeasing political parties, which ideally enables them to make impartial decisions based on their interpretation of the Constitution and the law. Furthermore, because justices do not have to secure reappointment or cater to shifting political landscapes, they are less likely to be swayed by public opinion, focusing instead on a long-term view of justice and governance.

The Counterargument

Despite these frequent criticisms, a lot has changed since the time of Alexander Hamilton. Term limits can also be argued to support judicial independence in ways that lifetime appointments may not.

Under a term-limited system, justices could still serve long enough. Eighteen years, as I'm in favor of, is more than enough time to maintain a sense of continuity and stability, while also promoting a periodic infusion of fresh perspectives. A term limit of this length would still insulate justices from short-term political pressures, allowing them to make impartial decisions without needing to consider reappointment.

Moreover, by implementing term limits, the Court would benefit from a system that reduces the impact of any one justice's ideological leanings over decades while weeding out external influence. Regular turnover would prevent any single justice from shaping constitutional interpretation for a prolonged period, offering a safeguard against the potential entrenchment of outdated views.

Thus, while lifetime tenure has traditionally been viewed as the optimal method for ensuring judicial independence, the implementation of term limits offers a balanced approach. By allowing justices to serve lengthy but finite terms, a term-limited system could preserve judicial independence, reduce potential ideological rigidity, and create a Supreme Court more reflective of contemporary values without sacrificing its core impartiality it was granted through the Constitution and subsequent legal precedents.

Some Fear The Appointment Process Would Become Even More Political

Another common argument against implementing term limits is the concern that more frequent vacancies could make the appointment process even more contentious and political. As we looked at in the previous chapter, opponents and skeptics worry that increased turnover would lead to a cycle of continuous confirmation hearings, potentially intensifying partisanship and conflict. These critics often argue that with predictable and regular vacancies, political parties would be motivated to place ideologically aligned judges on the Court, making the judiciary more vulnerable to partisan influences.

Currently, lifetime appointments mean that each vacancy holds significant weight, leading to intense political battles over nominees. Some have suggested that if term limits created regular vacancies, the process might become even more polarized. This would mean that term limits could lead each presidential election to feel like a referendum on the Supreme Court's future composition, which could further increase the influence of ideology and partisanship in the nomination process (*Pros and Cons of Potential Term Limits...*, 2014).

Additionally, each new justice could shift the Court's balance more quickly, prompting political groups to view judicial appointments as an opportunity to advance or secure specific ideological gains.

The Counterargument

Despite these concerns and the validity of some of the points, proponents of term limits argue that a carefully designed system could reduce, rather than exacerbate, political pressures. The proposed 2021 Supreme Court Term Limits and Regular Appointments Act, for instance, suggested 18-year terms with new appointments every two years.

Though the bill ultimately failed, an approach like this would address many concerns, as it would mean that each presidential term would see two Supreme Court nominations, creating a predictable and routine vacancy schedule. Such regularized appointments could help distribute influence over the Court's composition more evenly across administrations, reducing the ability of any single president to dramatically shift the Court's balance.

By spreading out the timing of vacancies, a future bill that borrows elements from the one proposed by Representative Khanna could decrease the high-stakes nature of individual nominations, lessening the need for intense partisan battles. Proponents contend that this would make the confirmation process less of a focal point in presidential elections, lowering the temperature around Supreme Court appointments.

Instead of aiming to "lock in" specific ideological outcomes, regular appointments would enable the Court's composition to evolve gradually, providing an opportunity for more measured shifts in judicial philosophy.

Despite These Doubts, The Time For Change is Now!

While concerns about judicial independence, continuity, and political influence are valid, they cannot obstruct necessary progress toward a more dynamic and accountable Supreme Court. The landscape of our society has transformed since the framers established lifetime appointments, and it's clear that the Court must also evolve if it is to truly serve the people in a fair and impartial manner.

The urgency for change has never been greater. The current system breeds political tension and stifles the regular infusion of perspectives essential to a responsive judiciary. Implementing term limits would help ensure the Supreme Court reflects the values of a living democracy, able to adapt to new social and legal realities. Now is the time to act; It's long past time to build a judiciary that embodies both stability and the capacity for growth, keeping it attuned to the needs of the nation.

You can help make this change a reality by educating yourself and others about the benefits of term limits, advocating for reform legislation, and supporting groups that work to modernize the Court. By lending your voice to this movement, you contribute to building a judiciary that better serves us all and aligns with the democratic ideals it was created to uphold.

Before We Move On

As we've explored, the case for Supreme Court term limits hinges on the principles of accountability, judicial independence, and the need for fresh perspectives in a constantly evolving society. While there are credible objections, the potential benefits—reduced political tension, a judiciary more in touch with contemporary issues, and an institution that evolves alongside the nation—are all compelling reasons for reform.

In the next chapter, we'll talk more about why these issues matter so much: public perception and trust. Ultimately, the Supreme Court's legitimacy depends on the public's faith in its role as a fair and impartial arbiter of justice. We'll learn how term limits could positively impact trust in the judiciary.

Chapter 8:

Looking at Public Perception and Trust

In recent years, public trust in the U.S. Supreme Court has reached alarmingly low levels. According to Gallup polling data, confidence in the Court dropped to just 27% in 2023, placing it among the least trusted American institutions (Saad, 2023). This trend reflects a broader decline in faith in branches of the government, but the judiciary's credibility faces unique challenges rooted in perceptions of partisanship and stagnation within its ranks.

Lifetime appointments for Supreme Court justices, once heralded as a safeguard of judicial independence, are increasingly viewed as a source of ideological entrenchment and disconnection from contemporary societal values. Landmark decisions in recent years have amplified public perception of the Court as a politically influenced body. As these rulings align more closely with the ideological leanings of long-serving justices, many Americans have grown skeptical of the Court's impartiality and role as a neutral arbiter of justice.

This chapter explores the critical importance of public trust in the judiciary. We'll look at how lifetime appointments have contributed to the erosion of confidence in the Supreme Court, explore the reasons behind this decline, and discuss how term limits could play a role in restoring trust. By understanding the public's growing disillusionment, we can chart a path forward to preserve the Court's legitimacy and its vital role in upholding democratic principles.

Public Perception of the Court

While this design of the Supreme Court was intended to insulate the judiciary from short-term public sentiment, it has increasingly been viewed as fueling an ideological disconnect. Research such as the SCOTUSPoll project led by Maya Sen of Harvard Kennedy School in 2020 provided insight into the alignment—or lack thereof—between public opinion and Court rulings. Through surveys of 2,000 Americans on contentious legal issues, the study revealed that while the Court often ruled in line with public sentiment on issues like LGBTQ+ rights and DACA protections for children of illegal immigrants, its overall decisions increasingly mirrored the ideological shifts of its members rather than consistent public expectations (Smith, 2020).

One example of this disconnect was seen two years later in the Supreme Court's 2022 decision in *Dobbs v. Jackson Women's Health Organization*. Overturning nearly 50 years of precedent set by *Roe*, the ruling removed the constitutional protection for abortion rights and returned regulatory authority to individual states. Public reaction was swift and polarized. For many Americans, this decision reinforced the perception that the Court was acting in accordance with the ideological leanings of its majority rather than respecting established legal precedents or broader societal consensus.

The *Dobbs* decision has come to be emblematic of the Court's perceived partisanship in recent years. Justice Samuel Alito, writing for the majority, argued that such decisions were not Constitutional matters, and should thereby be left up to each state. While supporters hailed this as a return to constitutional originalism, critics, including the dissenting justices, argued that the decision disregarded decades of reliance on *Roe v. Wade* and undermined the Court's legitimacy. Justice Stephen Breyer, in his dissent, warned that the ruling jeopardized public trust by appearing to be driven by the ideological composition of the Court rather than consistent legal reasoning.

Polling data immediately following the *Dobbs* ruling showed a staggering 25 percentage point drop in the Court's approval ratings among Democrats (Brenan, 2023), many members of that party viewing the decision as clearly politically motivated. While the views of members of one political should not be used to gauge an entire nation's sentiment, ongoing public opinion surveys conducted by the Pew Research Center continue to confirm that a majority of Americans support access to abortion, no matter their political affiliation (*Public Opinion on Abortion*, 2024).

The ruling fueled broader concerns that other long-standing rights, such as access to contraception or same-sex marriage, could be similarly endangered.

Eroding Public Confidence: Can The Court "Survive The Stench" of Politicization?

Justice Sotomayor's pointed remark during *Dobbs'* proceedings—that the Supreme Court, as an institution, might not "survive the stench" (Levendusky et al., 2024) of being perceived as political—highlighted real fears from within the ranks that its legitimacy was at risk. The ruling, made possible only by President Trump's appointees, Justices Kavanaugh and Coney Barrett, epitomized concerns that the Court's decisions are increasingly determined by partisan alignments rather than by an objective interpretation of the law (Levendusky et al., 2024).

The *Dobbs* decision did more than overturn a long-held legal precedent; it starkly divided public opinion along partisan lines. This polarization is unprecedented, as earlier studies (pre-*Dobbs*) had shown that both Democrats and Republicans viewed the Court as more neutral and removed from everyday political struggles than the other branches of government (Levendusky et al., 2024).

While Pre-*Dobbs*, Democrats actually expressed slightly higher confidence in the Court versus Republicans, Post-*Dobbs*, Republicans have tended to express greater trust in the Court's direction (Levendusky et al., 2024).

As we've seen throughout the chapters of this book, historically, the Supreme Court *was* regarded as a neutral institution, specifically designed to be isolated from the partisan political struggles that often define Congress and the presidency. Its perceived independence was central to its legitimacy, providing a critical check on the other branches of government.

However, this perception has changed. Recent surveys show a growing belief among Americans that the Court's decisions are influenced more by the ideologies of the appointing presidents than by adherence to constitutional principles (Levendusky et al., 2024). This shift in public opinion highlights how the Court's role in high-profile, politically charged cases has reshaped its image in the public eye.

This erosion of confidence poses significant risks for the Court's role in maintaining its legitimacy in the decades to come. As its decisions are increasingly viewed through a partisan lens, the public may become less willing to accept its rulings as legitimate or binding. This dynamic not only challenges the Court's authority but also complicates its ability to serve its intended function as a stabilizing force within the U.S. democratic system.

Restoring Trust Through Reform: It Is Possible!

Lifetime appointments, while originally conceived to safeguard judicial independence, have increasingly been viewed as driving detachment from the evolving preferences of the public.

Those of us in favor of reform argue that term limits would mitigate this disconnect by creating regular opportunities for new appointments, thus aligning the judiciary more closely with current legal and social priorities. But what about the other side and the high-stakes partisan battleground the Court is seen as being today?

Empirical research has confirmed the potential benefits of term limits in maintaining public trust. Studies done in the last decade have shown that Americans across all political affiliations broadly support the idea of updating the Court's composition to reflect the prevailing ideological and societal landscapes (Sen et al., 2020).

While Republicans amped up their approval of the Court post-*Dobbs*, polling prior to that ruling surprisingly revealed bipartisan support for term limits. According to a survey conducted before the *Dobbs* ruling, in 2021, 63% of Americans—including majorities of Democrats (71%), Republicans (60%), and Independents (64%)—favored imposing either term or age limits on justices (Ipsos, 2021).

This level of consensus around the issue points to a continued need for structural changes that increase accountability without compromising judicial independence. That same survey indicated that such reforms enjoy significantly more support than alternatives like court expansion, which garnered only 38% approval (Ipsos, 2021).

Viewed together, these numbers suggest that despite partisan divisions, Supreme Court reforms remain a viable possibility in the years and decades to come.

Before We Move On

Plummeting public trust in the Court represents a profound challenge for an institution that relies on its legitimacy to function effectively in a democracy. Now that we've explored today's troubling trust deficit by taking a closer look at public sentiment, it becomes clear that the path forward, from concept to implementation, is possible yet fraught with challenges.

In the next chapter, *The Road to Implementation*, we will delve into the legal, political, and procedural hurdles that must be navigated to make these reforms a reality. Understanding these obstacles is crucial to turning ideas for Court reform into actionable change, ensuring that the judiciary remains an important institution in American democracy.

Chapter 9:

The Road To Implementation

Implementing term limits would represent a monumental shift in the United States' judicial system, aiming to address public concerns about judicial accountability and ideological entrenchment. However, enacting such a reform would be far from a straightforward process. It would involve facing a rather complex web of legal, political, and procedural hurdles. The lifetime appointment of justices, enshrined in the Constitution and historically interpreted as giving the mandate for lifetime tenures, represents a clear barrier.

In this chapter, we'll examine the practical pathways to implementing term limits, beginning with the most direct yet arduous route: amending the Constitution. We'll also explore potential legislative and informal approaches that could achieve similar goals without the need for a constitutional amendment.

Finally, we'll assess the political feasibility of these reforms, considering the polarized political climate and growing public demand for change. Through this analysis, we can start to get an idea of the barriers and opportunities involved in realizing such an ambitious reform and start to prepare for the long road ahead of us.

The Constitutional Amendment Approach

Implementing term limits for Supreme Court justices would likely require a constitutional amendment to the "good Behaviour" clause of Article III (*U.S. Constitution - Article III*, 1787). Again, this has traditionally been interpreted as meaning a life tenure unless of course a Justice voluntarily resigns, retires, or is forcibly impeached and removed from the bench.

Only one U.S. Supreme Court Justice has ever been impeached in the entire history of the court (*Frequently Asked Questions: General Information*, 2019), so this is unlikely to happen again. Even in that one historical instance, the Justice in question, Samuel Chase, was still able to carry out his term.

Modifying the entrenched standard of Article III that essentially makes lifetime tenure the norm would likely require altering the Constitution in some way, as it's the keystone document that forms the structural foundation of judicial independence in the American government.

Article V of the Constitution outlines the process for amending the document. There are two primary pathways: The first, and historically the only method used, requires a two-thirds majority vote in both chambers of Congress, the House and the Senate (Columbia Law School, 2014; ArtV.1, Overview of Article V).

The second pathway calls for a constitutional convention. Regardless of the method used to propose an amendment, if the measure did pass Congress, it would then have to be ratified by three-quarters of the states (though this equates to an odd 37.5 states, we can assume in to mean 38 states) to become part of the Constitution (Columbia Law School, 2014; ArtV.1, Overview of Article V).

Historically, this process has proven to be both time-consuming and arduous. Since the Constitution's inception, only 27 amendments have been successfully ratified out of more than 33 proposed (*Overview of Article v, Amending the Constitution*, n.d.).

The most recent constitutional amendment, the 27th Amendment, which addresses congressional pay adjustments, stands as proof of the immense challenges inherent in amending the Constitution. First proposed in 1789, but not ratified until 1992, the amendment had an extraordinary journey, taking over 200 years from its proposal to its passing ("Twenty-Seventh Amendment," 2024). This example clearly demonstrates the procedural and temporal hurdles involved in constitutional reform, especially for changes as consequential as Supreme Court term limits.

As highlighted frequently in debates, while term limits might address issues like extended judicial tenure and strategic retirements, achieving the necessary consensus for such a constitutional change would be a formidable task, to say the least.

The safeguards of Article V emphasize the gravity of altering the nation's foundational document, making it a daunting task for those who support Court reforms that would require the alteration of Article III.

Alternative Approaches

Legislative Options

One alternative approach is that instead of amending the constitution, Congress could pursue legislative options to impose term limits for Supreme Court justices, such as laws establishing mandatory retirement ages or fixed terms through judicial appointments. Some scholars argue that such reforms might be feasible without a constitutional amendment, leveraging Congress's authority under Article III of the Constitution to regulate the judiciary (Wheeler, 2021).

Any potential legislative approach must contend with the Supreme Court's likely resistance to changes perceived as undermining judicial independence. These reforms could provide a more attainable pathway for addressing concerns about lifetime tenure, particularly in a political environment where constitutional amendments face steep hurdles (Wheeler, 2021).

Voluntary Informal Options

Establishing informal norms or precedents for judicial retirement or staggered terms could provide a pragmatic and flexible alternative to the complex process of constitutional amendments. Such an approach would involve presidents nominating justices with an informal understanding that they would retire after serving a specified number of years.

The idea is that this might create more predictable turnover on the Supreme Court without the need for binding legal mandates. While not codified, these norms could gradually shape expectations and practices, aligning with the broader goal of promoting judicial accountability and maintaining public trust in the Court.

This approach has several advantages. First, it avoids the lengthy and politically fraught process of passing constitutional amendments or significant legislation. Informal agreements, by their nature, are adaptable and could gain acceptance more quickly in a polarized environment. Secondly, this method is not without precedent. Other nations around the world, as we saw in Chapter 4, already have systems that promote judicial turnover through retirement ages or fixed terms without requiring constitutional changes, offering viable models for the U.S. to consider. Thirdly, such a method would balance flexibility with stability, ensuring the Court adapts over time while preserving its institutional independence.

However, the limitations of this strategy should also be acknowledged. Since these norms lack legal enforceability, they depend on voluntary adherence and could be easily disregarded by future administrations. Despite this, the political feasibility of establishing informal precedents may make it a realistic first step toward broader reform, especially in light of growing public support for changes to how justices serve their terms.

Assessing The Political Feasibility

The current political environment presents numerous challenges to enacting Supreme Court reforms, particularly those that propose term limits for justices. The ideological balance of the Court, already a contentious issue, creates some steep barriers to bipartisan support for reform. Efforts to impose term limits are often perceived as attempts to shift the Court's ideological leanings, further deepening partisan divisions (Eisen & Matsuki, 2022).

Resistance to Reforms From Conservatives and Liberals Alike

The polarized nature of American politics, and the recent move rightward, with the election of Donald Trump and a GOP-dominated congress means that both major parties will likely be cautious about endorsing any reforms that could alter the composition of the Court in ways that may disadvantage them on other legislation.

This resistance will likely be exacerbated by the heightened partisanship surrounding any new judicial appointments, as seen in the contentious confirmations of Justices Kavanaugh and Brown Jackson. These ongoing dynamics underscore the difficulty of achieving consensus on judicial reforms within the current political landscape.

Despite these obstacles, public sentiment could be a critical lever for change. As we looked at previously, polls have historically indicated substantial public support for term limits, with two-thirds (66%) of Americans still favoring such measures according to a recent Washington Post poll (Raji, 2024).

There Is Still Hope

If this public dissatisfaction continues to build, it might eventually exert enough pressure to force lawmakers to engage with reform proposals, even in the face of significant partisan challenges. However, without broad bipartisan support, implementing term limits or similar reforms remains an uphill battle, and with the recent GOP sweep of the White House and Congress, the changing political tides may swallow up any forward momentum.

Public pressure has proven to be a potentially decisive force in driving Supreme Court reform, particularly as confidence in the institution continues to wane. While the overturning of *Roe v. Wade* was deeply upsetting for many who support womens' right to choose, it exemplifies a broader trend of controversial rulings that many Americans perceive as misaligned with public opinion, further eroding trust in the Court's neutrality.

Polling data conducted in the aftermath highlighted the extent of public discontent. At that time, only 48% of Americans viewed the Supreme Court favorably in the wake of the Dobbs decision, marking a sharp decline from previous years. Simultaneously, support for reforms such as term limits was growing, with 67% of Americans expressing approval for such changes (Eisen & Matsuki, 2022), a figure which has remained more or less stable according to the recent 2024 Washington Post poll we looked at in the previous section (Raji, 2024).

Widespread dissatisfaction with systems and institutions builds momentum for reform. Public advocacy and organized campaigns can continue to place pressure on elected officials to prioritize reform, especially as these initiatives are framed as necessary steps to restore accountability and align the Court with evolving societal values. Let's not forget that the increasing polarization of judicial appointments has further galvanized public interest in structural changes, as Americans seek a judiciary that's independent and impartial while addressing the issues that matter to them.

While political feasibility remains a significant hurdle, the combination of public support and diminishing institutional trust may still be conducive to an environment ripe for incremental reforms. The role of the public in reshaping the Court cannot be understated, particularly as citizens demand a judiciary that reflects democratic principles and contemporary expectations.

Before We Move On

As we've explored in this chapter, the road to implementing term limits for Supreme Court justices is fraught with some daunting challenges. From the monumental task of amending the Constitution to exploring alternative legislative and informal strategies, the journey is both complex and deeply rooted in political realities. Yet, the growing public support for reform, coupled with the urgent need to restore trust in the judiciary, points to a viable path forward for reforms.

Our discussions on political feasibility and alternative approaches underscore a key point: Achieving meaningful reform requires both adaptability and openness. Any efforts will have to reach across party lines. Incremental changes, driven by public advocacy and bipartisan dialogue, may pave the way for more transformative solutions. However, the nuances of the kinds of political and legal landscapes we find ourselves immersed in today must not be underestimated.

In the next chapter, *What a Term-Limited Court Might Look Like*, we shift from the procedural hurdles of reform to the possibilities it could unlock. We'll look at how a term-limited Supreme Court might work toward building greater judicial independence, becoming more adaptable to evolving societal values, and regaining the trust of the American public. By envisioning the Court of the future, the court *we the people* want, we can gain a clearer picture of what's at stake and what the tangible benefits of reform might be.

Chapter 10:

What a Term-Limited Court Might Look Like

As we've seen throughout the chapters of this book, despite its problems, the Supreme Court stands as a key component of the American democratic system, wielding an extraordinary amount of influence over the nation's laws, freedoms, and fundamental rights.

The Court today is much like the country itself—beset by challenges that threaten to erode its legitimacy and strain public trust. Life tenure for justices—drafted as part of the Constitution at a time when life expectancy was far shorter—has contributed to a system that is often out of sync with modern realities.

A Supreme Court like the one we have today, where justices serve for decades way past other lingering policies of the administrations that appointed them, risks becoming an institution frozen in time, unable to adapt to the rapidly shifting societal and legal landscapes we face in the 21st century and beyond.

What if we could work toward guaranteeing a Court that serves its original intent while also allowing fresh perspectives to flow regularly into its deliberations—a Court that evolves with the people it serves, its decisions informed by the most current societal values and legal reasoning? This is the promise of term limits for Supreme Court justices: A system that balances the need for continuity and institutional memory with the undeniable benefits of periodic judicial renewal.

The Court *can* be transformed into a dynamic, adaptable, and representative institution, either through term limits or other similar reforms. Though certainly challenging to implement, as we already saw in the previous chapter's discussion, none of these ideas are overly idealistic "what ifs"; they are, in fact, largely attainable reforms that, if thoughtfully implemented, could revitalize the judiciary and reaffirm its role as an impartial arbiter of justice.

The current life tenure system can lead to stagnation, where justices, entrenched in their positions for decades, are prone to drift away from contemporary realities. Term limits would counteract this by ensuring regular turnover. This type of predictable cycle would allow society to adapt to the rhythm of judicial appointments, tempering political tensions.

More than just a mechanism for change, term limits would infuse the judiciary with new energy and ideas. Each generation brings fresh perspectives on issues ranging from technology and privacy to climate change and civil rights. By enabling regular judicial renewal, term limits would ensure that the Court remains in step with societal progress rather than perpetually anchored in the past.

The Promise To Heal Political Hostilities

Today's high-stakes presidential and congressional races have made Supreme Court confirmation battles just as contentious; they stand today as examples of what's essentially partisan warfare. The rare opportunity to shape the Court's composition for decades means that the stakes are even higher for court appointments, as they have lasting implications for the nation's laws and governance that far exceed presidential election cycles and limits and the accompanying Congressional turnover. Term limits could defuse this tension.

By instituting regular and predictable vacancies, the confirmation process would lose much of its current intensity. Each administration would have a fair and consistent opportunity to appoint justices, reducing the incentive for political trickery.

Term limits promise to eliminate the strategic retirements that have further politicized the Court. No longer would justices be able to time their departures to align with ideologically compatible presidents. Instead, the institution would operate on a clear, impartial schedule, reducing the perception of the Court as an extension of partisan interests.

Toward A More Representative Bench

The demographics and values of the United States are not static; they evolve continually. Yet the Supreme Court often lags behind these changes, constrained by the long tenures of its justices.

A term-limited Court would be better equipped to reflect the nation's diversity—not just in race, gender, and socioeconomic background but in thought, philosophy, and approach to justice. Regular turnover would allow the Court to adjust more quickly to demographic shifts and societal changes, ensuring that it remains a truly representative institution.

This is not just about appearances; it's about legitimacy. A Court perceived as ideologically out of step with the majority of Americans risks shedding the public's trust even further, which as we've already seen is at concerning levels. By allowing for periodic rebalancing, term limits would help the Court maintain its relevance and its foundational commitment to justice for all.

A Just Vision for the Future

The case for term limits isn't just about fixing what's broken; it's about envisioning what could be. A term-limited Supreme Court would be more dynamic, more representative, and less entangled in partisan strife.

It would reclaim its standing as an institution that inspires trust rather than suspicion, and respect rather than skepticism. As we explore the potentials and possibilities of these types of reform, let's take a moment to remember that no government institution, including the Supreme Court, exists in a vacuum. Far from being completely insulated, it is in fact shaped by the people it serves, and it can—and must—evolve to meet their needs; otherwise, it risks completely losing legitimacy in their eyes.

Toward A More Dynamic Court

A term-limited Supreme Court presents a compelling opportunity to infuse the judiciary with a renewed sense of adaptability and responsiveness. As the nation grapples with political polarization and the rapid pace of societal and technological change, it is worth considering how regular turnover among justices might improve the Court's prospects for attaining alignment with contemporary realities.

Turnover Matters

This prolonged influence of justices who serve 30 years or even more risks disconnecting the judiciary from contemporary norms and challenges. Regular judicial turnover, facilitated by term limits, would ensure a steady influx of fresh perspectives and legal interpretations.

An 18-year term limit, such as the one I support, would likely provide enough time for justices to gain experience and leave a mark without overstaying their relevance. Under this type of model, new appointees would rotate in regularly, allowing the Court to adapt more swiftly to societal shifts. By breaking the cycle of justices remaining entrenched for decades, the Court would more effectively reflect modern legal and cultural realities.

Preserving Tradition While Meeting Future Needs

While the introduction of term limits would help bring in a more dynamic judiciary, it's equally important to consider the Court's institutional memory and stability. Critics of term limits often raise concerns about destabilizing the judiciary, arguing that too much turnover could disrupt the Court's ability to build on legal precedents. However, an 18-year tenure strikes this careful balance, allowing justices to establish continuity in their jurisprudence while ensuring that no individual justice wields influence for an excessive period.

Let's not forget that historically, the average tenure of justices during the first two centuries of the Court was around 15 years (Fisher, 2022). This natural rhythm was disrupted in recent decades as advancements in healthcare extended life expectancy and presidents began appointing younger justices to maximize their influence. Term limits would restore a more traditional cycle of judicial service, ensuring both renewal and the preservation of legal stability.

In a world where societal norms and technological landscapes are evolving at an ever-accelerating pace, the Supreme Court must be equipped to address novel legal challenges effectively. From navigating the implications of artificial intelligence to addressing complex social issues, the judiciary faces increasingly complex and nuanced cases. Term limits would allow the Court to respond to such shifts with greater agility, as justices appointed in closer proximity to these developments would bring firsthand understanding of emerging ethical and legal issues around new technologies.

Injecting Energy and Vigor Into the Most Crucial Rulings

Another advantage of term limits is their potential to align justices' tenure with their peak professional performance. Currently, the push to appoint increasingly younger justices incentivizes presidents to prioritize longevity over experience. Term limits would reduce this pressure, allowing presidents to select nominees with a greater emphasis on qualifications and expertise. As a result, justices would likely serve during the most productive years of their careers, bringing a combination of wisdom and vigor to their roles (Fisher, 2022).

By imposing limits on tenure, the Court could avoid situations where justices continue to serve despite declining health or acuity, ensuring a judiciary that remains robust and effective. This would also address public concerns about the impartiality and effectiveness of justices serving well into advanced age, which, as we saw previously, can have an impact on confidence in the Court's decisions.

A Vision of the Future: A More Dynamic Court Is Possible!

Imagine a Supreme Court that thrives on a steady infusion of fresh ideas, where justices bring contemporary perspectives to the bench, and their contributions align with the challenges of a rapidly evolving society. In this future, the Court operates as a dynamic institution, reflecting the nation's current values while retaining the wisdom of its historical precedents.

Justices would serve for 18 years, and 18 only—just long enough to develop expertise and make significant contributions, but not so long that their views risk becoming disconnected from the realities of the modern world.

Every presidential administration has an equal opportunity to shape the judiciary, nominating justices at regular intervals, free from the high-stakes unpredictability that currently dominates the appointment process. This predictability reduces the partisan rancor that has plagued Supreme Court confirmations, fostering a calmer, more respectful approach to judicial nominations.

In this future vision, the Court mirrors the diversity and evolving demographics of the nation it serves. Regular turnover ensures that the bench consistently reflects contemporary America, incorporating voices from varied backgrounds and perspectives. The 18-year term limit safeguards against ideological stagnation, enabling the Court to stay attuned to the nation's shifting cultural, technological, and legal landscapes.

Globally, the U.S. would finally join the ranks of almost every other constitutional democracy in the world, recognizing the value of judicial term limits, aligning with best practices while maintaining its own principles of justice and impartiality. The Court would no longer be seen as an institution disconnected from the lives of everyday Americans but as one that evolves alongside them, building trust and legitimacy through its structure and decisions. The court's approval rating would attain healthy levels.

This future is within reach. An 18-year term-limited Supreme Court offers a vision of balance: between continuity and change, independence and accountability, tradition and modernization. Such a reform could transform the judiciary into a more dynamic and responsive institution, ready to meet the demands of the present while upholding the principles that matter to the American people.

Reducing Political Hostilities

We have to face the reality that, under the current system, Supreme Court vacancies are infrequent. Some presidents, including Jimmy Carter, never even had the chance to nominate a justice (Congressional Research Service, 2022), while others have had the benefit of having multiple opportunities to reshape the Court during their terms.

The rarity of vacancies has incentivized strategic political maneuvers. For instance, in 2016, the Republican-led Senate would not budge in their blocking of President Obama's nomination of Merrick Garland, citing the fact that the next presidential election was just months away (Elving, 2018). In 2020, however, the same Senate expedited the confirmation of Amy Coney Barrett weeks before Election Day (Sprunt, 2020). Double standards like these, aside from being unfair, erode public trust and deepen political divisions. This makes reform all the more essential.

The Right Solution

Term limits are the right solution because the regularity of turnover would ensure that every presidential term includes two Supreme Court nominations, regardless of unforeseen vacancies. By eliminating the element of chance, term limits would lower the stakes of each nomination and distribute appointment opportunities more equitably among presidents.

Predictable vacancies would shift the focus from ideological domination to consistent, measured contributions to the Court. With every administration guaranteed a set number of appointments, the urgency to stack the Court with ideologically extreme candidates would diminish. Presidents could focus on nominating well-qualified jurists, knowing that their influence on the Court would neither be disproportionately large nor entirely absent.

Strategic Retirements No More!

Currently, justices can choose when to retire, often timing their departures to align with favorable political conditions. This practice introduces an additional layer of partisanship, as justices may remain on the bench longer than they would otherwise or retire prematurely to ensure a like-minded successor.

As we talked about in Chapter 5, Justice Ruth Bader Ginsburg refused to step down during President Obama's tenure, only to pass away during the Trump administration, allowing her replacement to shift the Court significantly to the right.

Under a term-limited system, justices would not need to strategize their retirements. Their terms would end predictably, and their successors would be appointed on a set schedule. This change would reduce the perception of the Court as a political instrument, and would likely be conducive to building a greater sense of impartiality and public trust.

Lowering the Temperature of Confirmation Battles

The predictability of term limits would also alleviate the political pressure surrounding confirmation hearings. Currently, the confirmation process has devolved into a spectacle, with nominees subjected to grueling public scrutiny and partisan attacks. These battles not only damage the credibility of the Court but also may discourage highly qualified candidates from accepting nominations.

With regular vacancies, the confirmation process could become more routine and less contentious. Senators would have fewer incentives to block or expedite nominations based on partisan considerations, knowing that appointments occur on a predictable schedule. Over time, this could lead to a cultural shift where judicial qualifications take precedence over ideological battles, restoring decorum and professionalism to the process.

A Clear Vision of a Less Divisive Future

Imagine a United States Supreme Court transformed into an institution where each administration contributes to its evolution without overshadowing it. Over two decades, with term limits in place, the Court could shed its image as a battleground for ideological dominance, emerging instead as a symbol of balance, fairness, and adaptability. This shift could ripple through society, gradually eroding the bitter divisions that have marked American politics for decades.

In this less divisive future, the public's trust in the judiciary would be restored. The lifetime tenure that once tied justices to the political ideologies of the presidents who appointed them is replaced by a predictable rhythm of transitions. Americans would begin to see the Court not as a static institution beholden to the past but as a living body capable of reflecting the nation's evolving values.

The political sphere, too, would feel the transformative effects of this reform. Senate confirmation hearings, freed from the shadow of lifetime appointments, focus less on partisan loyalty and more on legal qualifications and jurisprudence. Political parties, knowing they will have recurring opportunities to shape the Court, step back from the unfair tactics that once defined their battles over nominations.

The fever pitch of hostility surrounding appointments would hopefully cool down and be replaced by a calmer, more deliberate approach. In this atmosphere, governance becomes the priority, and the legislative and executive branches regain their focus on collaboration and effective policy-making.

If the Supreme Court goes through these reforms, it could become a model of balance and renewal. Other institutions could begin to follow suit. Efforts to implement similar reforms in lower federal courts and other areas of government could gain momentum, touching every level of governance.

The idea of regular turnover and shared responsibility fosters a culture of accountability and innovation, where leaders are less entrenched and more responsive to the needs of the people. Why not propose term limits on congress members next? The possibilities here are endless!

Toward A More Representative Judiciary

Imagine that the year is 2044, and term limits for the United States Supreme Court have already transformed the judiciary into a vibrant and responsive institution that reflects the nation it serves. The change, muted at first, has ushered in profound benefits for American democracy, reshaping the Court's role in ways that strengthen the public's trust and the nation's legal system.

In this imagined but plausible future, the judiciary is no longer perceived as an enclave of entrenched ideologies. With 18-year nonrenewable terms in place, justices rotate in and out of service on a predictable schedule, ensuring that each presidential administration has a meaningful opportunity to contribute to the Court's composition.

The result is a bench that reflects the diversity of America, not just in terms of demographics but also in professional experiences and generational perspectives. Gone are the days when the Court's makeup seemed frozen in time, tethered to the political and cultural values of an earlier era. Instead, the Court now evolves alongside the nation, making it a living institution that remains attuned to the realities of modern life.

This regular turnover has not only broadened the range of viewpoints represented on the Court but has also invigorated its decision-making. Justices bring with them fresh insights on issues like artificial intelligence, climate resilience, and the digital economy—areas where the law must adapt quickly to rapid societal change.

Decisions from this forward-looking Court resonate deeply with the public, who see in its rulings a reflection of their contemporary struggles and aspirations. Legal interpretations no longer feel like relics of a bygone age but instead address the pressing challenges of today and tomorrow.

The broader societal impact of these changes cannot be overstated. Citizens, seeing themselves better represented in the judiciary under such reforms, would likely feel a renewed sense of trust in the rule of law. This trust extends to the Court's decisions, which, while not always popular, would be accepted as legitimate by a public that recognizes the Court as an impartial arbiter of justice, as it was originally intended to be.

Okay, sounds great, right? But how are we going to pull this off. This is where public advocacy comes in.

The Role of Public Advocacy: Today's Movements Pushing for Reform

Public advocacy has become an essential driver in the movement for Supreme Court reform, with organizations, think tanks, and scholars from across the political spectrum uniting around the idea of implementing term limits.

A variety of advocacy groups aim to address growing concerns about partisanship, judicial accountability, and public trust in the judiciary by promoting reforms that ensure the Court remains dynamic, impartial, and reflective of contemporary values.

Brennan Center for Justice

The Brennan Center for Justice, based at New York University School of Law, is a nonpartisan institute in law and public policy that advocates for democracy, justice, and the rule of law. Known for its rigorous research and public education initiatives, the Brennan Center has been at the forefront of the term limits movement, producing studies and reports that highlight the benefits of regular judicial turnover.

The organization's work emphasizes the importance of restoring public trust in the judiciary and curbing the partisanship that has increasingly defined Supreme Court nominations. Through advocacy, public campaigns, and legislative proposals, the Brennan Center aims to bring this issue to the forefront of national debate.

Federalist Society

The Federalist Society is a conservative and libertarian organization that plays a rather unique role in the conversation around Supreme Court reform. While traditionally focused on promoting a textualist and originalist interpretation of the Constitution, some members of the organization have in fact supported term limits as a way to depoliticize judicial appointments and enhance the judiciary's independence.

Prominent scholars associated with the Federalist Society have argued that predictable, staggered appointments could reduce the high-stakes battles over the Court's ideological composition and ensure a steady infusion of new perspectives (Fisher, 2022).

American Academy of Arts and Sciences

The American Academy of Arts and Sciences, a multidisciplinary research institute, has also lent its voice to the term limits movement. In its 2023 report, *The Case for Supreme Court Term Limits* ("Supreme Court Term Limits," 2023), the Academy proposed a system where justices would serve for 18 years, emphasizing the historical median tenure of justices and the need for regular turnover.

The proposal is rooted in extensive research and comparative analysis, drawing on examples from other democracies where limited judicial terms have enhanced both independence and accountability. By engaging experts across disciplines, the Academy offers a balanced perspective on how term limits could be implemented without compromising judicial integrity.

National Constitution Center

The National Constitution Center, a nonpartisan organization dedicated to constitutional education and debate, has also contributed to the term limits discussion. The Center provides a forum for scholars, lawmakers, and the public to explore reforms that align with the Constitution's principles while addressing modern challenges.

Its initiatives often feature debates and workshops where term limits are examined as a means of modernizing the judiciary and mitigating political polarization.

Fix the Court

Fix the Court is a grassroots advocacy group focused on increasing transparency and accountability in the judiciary. The organization has been a vocal proponent of Supreme Court term limits, frequently citing the need to align the Court's operations with modern expectations of governance.

Through media campaigns and public outreach, Fix the Court educates citizens about the benefits of reform and pressures lawmakers to take action. The group also advocates for other reforms, such as a binding code of ethics for justices and more transparent financial disclosures.

Center for American Progress

The Center for American Progress (CAP), a progressive policy think tank, has also joined the chorus of voices supporting judicial term limits. CAP frames term limits as a necessary step to reduce the influence of political agendas on the judiciary and to ensure that the Court evolves with the nation.

The organization's reports and advocacy efforts highlight the dangers of lifetime appointments, particularly when coupled with the increasing polarization of American politics.

How You Can Get Involved

For those of you who are inspired to take action in the movement for Supreme Court term limits, there are numerous ways to get involved, even without a background in public policy or law. The advocacy organizations we looked at in this chapter, online resources, and even local grassroots initiatives all provide accessible avenues for citizens to contribute to this important reform.

If you want to get involved locally, reaching out to your elected officials is a powerful way to advocate for change. Writing letters, making phone calls, or attending town halls to voice your support for Supreme Court reform ensures that this issue remains a priority for policymakers. Personalized communication can be particularly impactful, as representatives often consider the opinions of their constituents when shaping their legislative agendas.

If you have the resources to do so, consider contributing to fundraising efforts for organizations working on this issue. Donations help sustain their campaigns, fund research, and expand their ability to reach lawmakers and the public. Many groups offer transparent breakdowns of how contributions are used, ensuring that your support directly impacts the push for reform.

Lastly, educating yourself and others is a crucial step in bringing on change. Online resources from the groups we looked at earlier offer a wealth of information to build your understanding of judicial reform. By becoming knowledgeable about the issue, you can better articulate its importance and inspire others to join the movement.

Getting involved in the fight for Supreme Court term limits doesn't require a background in law or politics—just a commitment to strengthening democracy and ensuring fairness in the judiciary. Through education, advocacy, and community engagement, individuals can play a vital role in this transformative effort, helping to create a judiciary that better reflects and serves the American people.

Conclusion

As we bring this book to a close, it is worth reflecting on the central themes of this book and the profound implications they hold for American democracy.

As the apex of the American judicial system, the Supreme Court was intended to be a guardian of fairness and impartiality, a steady hand guiding the nation through the complexities of constitutional interpretation. However, the modern challenges of partisanship and lifetime tenure, and the mounting stakes of each nomination, have skewed the Court's role and public perception. It no longer feels like a neutral arbiter but a battleground for ideological dominance, with consequences that permeate every corner of society.

While there are certainly valid concerns about the implementation and effects of term limits, the overwhelming evidence suggests that they offer a practical, balanced solution to restore trust, accountability, and adaptability in the judiciary.

As you've read these pages, you now know that the type of reform we need isn't just about imposing restrictions; it's about recalibrating the Court to better serve the people, aligning it with the democratic values and principles it was designed to uphold.

The case for term limits is grounded in three key pillars: fairness, accountability, and modernization.

Fairness

Fairness demands that every president, regardless of timing or luck, has an equal opportunity to shape the judiciary, reducing the disproportionate influence of a single administration.

Accountability

Accountability ensures that justices remain connected to the society they serve, with regular turnover preventing ideological stagnation and fostering decisions that reflect contemporary values.

Modernization

Modernization acknowledges that the judiciary must evolve alongside the nation, addressing new challenges such as technology, climate change, and social justice with fresh perspectives.

Why The Benefits Outweigh the Risks

As we've seen, critics of term limits have raised concerns about potential instability, the risk of politicizing appointments, and the challenge of maintaining judicial independence. These are important considerations, but they do not outweigh the systemic benefits. Regular, predictable turnover would bring stability, not chaos, to the Court, ensuring a steady influx of new ideas without compromising its foundational role.

The politicization of appointments, far from being exacerbated, would likely diminish as the stakes of each individual nomination decrease. And judicial independence, safeguarded by nonrenewable terms and continued financial security for justices, would remain intact.

Moreover, term limits address a pressing reality: the increasing disconnection between a lifetime-tenured Court and the rapidly evolving society it governs. Without this reform, we risk perpetuating a system that places disproportionate power in the hands of a select few, chosen decades ago, whose perspectives may no longer align with the nation's trajectory.

For The Future's Sake

Now, let us take a moment to imagine an alternative future, one where no reforms are made. The advancements in life extension technologies and biohacking, coupled with the integration of Advanced Neural Networks (ANNs), may soon enable individuals to live—and remain cognitively active—for centuries.

In this world, the prospect of justices serving for 300 years or more becomes a chilling reality. Picture a Supreme Court frozen in time, its members shaped by the political, social, and cultural contexts of centuries past, wielding influence over a society unrecognizable from their own formative experiences.

Is this the judiciary we want? A Court that becomes more of an oligarchic relic than a responsive, democratic institution? If the arguments presented in this book have resonated, the answer is a resounding no.

The time to act is now—before technological advancements render the problem of lifetime tenure not just challenging but insurmountable. By implementing term limits today, we can ensure that the Court remains an institution grounded in justice, fairness, and adaptability, rather than an unchanging monument to the past.

You Too Can Fight For Change!

As a reader, you've already taken an important first step by engaging with these ideas and exploring the ins and outs of Supreme Court reform. Now, it's time to turn that awareness into action. Whether by joining activist groups, contacting your representatives, or educating others in your community through social media, your voice matters. Reforming the Supreme Court is not a task for legal experts or policymakers alone; it is a collective effort that requires the participation of informed citizens who care about the future of democracy.

Talk to your friends and family about the importance of term limits. Share what you've learned in this book, and encourage others to consider how these reforms could strengthen the judiciary and, by extension, the nation. If this book has inspired you or given you new insights, consider leaving a review on Amazon to help others discover its message. Better yet, pass it along to someone who might find it valuable—together, we can expand the conversation and build momentum for change.

Thank you for taking the time to learn more about this critical issue. The fact that you've read to the end of this book speaks to your dedication to fairness, accountability, and the principles of democracy. Your continued engagement and interest attest to the power informed citizens can have when they make the bold choice to drive progress and shape the institutions that govern us rather than sit back and do nothing.

As you close this book, remember that change is possible—but it requires action. The fight for term limits is ultimately a fight for a judiciary that serves the people, adapts to the times, and embodies the values of justice and equality. Together, we can make this vision a reality. Let us not delay, for the stakes are high, and the future of democracy depends on the steps we take today.

References

About the Supreme Court. (n.d.). Administrative Office of the U.S. Courts. https://www.uscourts.gov/about-federal-courts/educational-resources/about-educational-outreach/activity-resources/about

Advances in modern medicine affects Supreme Court. (2018, September 6). Harvard Medical School. https://hcp.hms.harvard.edu/news/advances-modern-medicine-affects-supreme-court

Albers, P. (n.d.). Performance indicators and evaluation for judges and courts. In *Council of Europe.* https://rm.coe.int/performance-indicators-and-evaluation-for-judges-and-courts-dr-pim-alb/16807907b0

Americans' views of 2024 election news: Most Americans are following the election closely, though roughly half say it's hard to know what's true. (2023, July 20). Pew Research Center. https://www.pewresearch.org/journalism/2024/10/10/americans-views-of-2024-election-news/

Armaly, M. T. (2018). Politicized nominations and public attitudes toward the Supreme Court in the polarization era. *The Justice System Journal, 39*(3), 193–209. https://www.jstor.org/stable/26595677

Armaly, M. T., & Lane, E. A. (2022). Politicized battles: How vacancies and partisanship influence support for the Supreme Court. *American Politics Research*, 1532673X2110642. https://doi.org/10.1177/1532673x211064299

Bailey, R. (2024, January 8). *Why is U.S. life expectancy declining? Guns, germs, and drugs*. Reason.com. https://reason.com/2024/01/08/guns-germs-and-drugs-are-largely-responsible-for-the-decline-in-u-s-life-expectancy/

Bannon, A., & Milov-Cordoba, M. (2023, September 20). *Supreme court term limits*. Brennan Center for Justice. https://www.brennancenter.org/our-work/policy-solutions/supreme-court-term-limits

Barak, A. (1998). The role of the Supreme Court in a democracy. *Israel Studies*, *3*(2), 6–29. https://doi.org/10.2979/isr.1998.3.2.6

Basaraba, S. (2012, September 18). *A guide to longevity throughout history, from the prehistoric onward*. Verywell Health. https://www.verywellhealth.com/longevity-throughout-history-2224054

Berman, L., Murphy, B. A., Brown, N., & Gershon, S. (2023). *Approaching democracy*. https://doi.org/10.4324/9781003303992

Biskupic, J. (2024, July 31). *Exclusive: How Samuel Alito got canceled from the Supreme Court social media majority*. CNN. https://edition.cnn.com/2024/07/31/politics/samuel-alito-supreme-court-netchoice-social-media-biskupic/index.html

Bomboy, S. (2023, June 30). *Significant Supreme Court cases in the 2022-2023 term.* National Constitution Center. https://constitutioncenter.org/blog/significant-supreme-court-cases-in-the-2022-2023-term

Bonica, A., & Sen, M. (2021). Estimating judicial ideology. *The Journal of Economic Perspectives, 35*(1), 97–118. https://www.jstor.org/stable/27008016

Brenan, M. (2023, September 29). *Views of Supreme Court remain near record lows.* Gallup. https://news.gallup.com/poll/511820/views-supreme-court-remain-near-record-lows.aspx

Brenan, M. (2024, July 30). *Approval of U.S. Supreme Court stalled near historical low.* Gallup. https://news.gallup.com/poll/647834/approval-supreme-court-stalled-near-historical-low.aspx

Buchanan, M. (2020). The need for Supreme Court term limits. In *The White House.* https://www.whitehouse.gov/wp-content/uploads/2021/08/CAP-Appendix.pdf

Burke, I. (2024, August 9). *A critique of Biden's proposal for Supreme Court term limits.* Jurist. https://www.jurist.org/commentary/2024/08/a-critique-of-bidens-proposal-for-supreme-court-term-limits/

City and county of San Francisco v. Environmental Protection Agency. (n.d.). SCOTUSblog. https://www.scotusblog.com/case-files/cases/city-and-county-of-san-francisco-v-environmental-protection-agency/

The composition of constitutional courts European commission for democracy through law. (1997). Council of Europe. https://www.venice.coe.int/webforms/documents/default.aspx?pdffile=CDL-STD(1997)020-e

Congressional Research Service. (2022). Supreme court nominations, 1789 to 2020: Actions by the Senate, the judiciary committee, and the president. In *US Congress.* https://crsreports.congress.gov/product/pdf/RL/RL33225

Cooper, T., Dworkin, A., Hosmer-Quint, D., & Pescovitz, A. (2022, January 20). *Retiring life tenure: On term limits and regular appointments at the Supreme Court.* Cardozo Law Review. https://cardozolawreview.com/retiring-life-tenure-on-term-limits-and-regular-appointments-at-the-supreme-court/

The court and constitutional interpretation. (2023). Supreme Court of the United States. https://www.supremecourt.gov/about/constitutional.aspx

The court as an institution. (2019). Supreme Court of the United States. https://www.supremecourt.gov/about/institution.aspx

"Court packing": Legislative control over the size of the Supreme Court. (2020). In *CRS Reports.* https://crsreports.congress.gov/product/pdf/LSB/LSB10562

Court role and structure. (2023). United States Courts. https://www.uscourts.gov/about-federal-courts/court-role-and-structure

Customary law. (2024). Judiciaries Worldwide. https://judiciariesworldwide.fjc.gov/customary-law

De Witte, M. (2024, February 14). *How political parties have changed over time.* Stanford University. https://news.stanford.edu/stories/2024/02/political-parties-changed-time

Debusmann Jr., B. (n.d.). *How the Supreme Court came to dominate the US political debate.* BBC. https://www.bbc.com/news/articles/crg4rz6zedyo

DeSilver, D. (2016, February 26). *Long supreme court vacancies used to be more common.* Pew Research Center. https://www.pewresearch.org/short-reads/2016/02/26/long-supreme-court-vacancies-used-to-be-more-common/

Dobbs v. Jackson women's health organization. (2022a). National Constitution Center. https://constitutioncenter.org/the-constitution/supreme-court-case-library/dobbs-v-jackson-womens-health-organization

Dobbs v. Jackson women's health organization. (2022b, June 24). SCOTUSblog. https://www.scotusblog.com/case-files/cases/dobbs-v-jackson-womens-health-organization/

Duignan, B. (2024, October 29). *Neil Gorsuch.* Encyclopedia Britannica. https://www.britannica.com/biography/Neil-Gorsuch

Eisen, N., & Matsuki, S. (2022, September 26). *Term limits—a way to tackle the Supreme Court's crisis of legitimacy*. Brookings. https://www.brookings.edu/articles/term-limits-a-way-to-tackle-the-supreme-courts-crisis-of-legitimacy/

Elving, R. (2018, June 29). *What happened with Merrick Garland in 2016 and why it matters now*. NPR. https://www.npr.org/2018/06/29/624467256/what-happened-with-merrick-garland-in-2016-and-why-it-matters-now

The federal court system. (2016). University of Central Florida. https://pressbooks.online.ucf.edu/amnatgov/chapter/the-federal-court-system/

Federal judiciary. (n.d.). Legal Information Institute. https://www.law.cornell.edu/wex/federal_judiciary

Fisher, J. (2022, July 21). *The Supreme Court reform that could actually win bipartisan support*. Politico. https://www.politico.com/news/magazine/2022/07/21/supreme-court-reform-term-limits-00046883

Frequently asked questions (FAQ). (2001, January 1). Supreme Court of Canada. https://www.scc-csc.ca/contact/faq/qa-qr-eng.aspx

Frequently asked questions: General information. (2019). Supreme Court of the United States. https://www.supremecourt.gov/about/faq_general.aspx

Fritze, J. (2024, April 27). *How Justice Amy Coney Barrett drove the Supreme Court's debate on abortion and Trump immunity*. CNN Politics. https://edition.cnn.com/2024/04/27/politics/amy-coney-barrett-supreme-court-immunity-idaho-abortion/index.html

Ginsburg, T. (2021). Term limits and turnover on the U.S. Supreme Court: A comparative view: Testimony for the presidential commission on the Supreme Court. In *The White House*. https://www.whitehouse.gov/wp-content/uploads/2021/07/Ginsburg-Testimony.pdf

Gira Grant, M. (2024, March 7). *Who exactly is behind the Supreme Court's big mifepristone case?* The New Republic. https://newrepublic.com/article/179626/mifepristone-abortion-supreme-court-alliance-hippocratic-medicine

Glossip v. Oklahoma. (2024, October 9). SCOTUSblog. https://www.scotusblog.com/case-files/cases/glossip-v-oklahoma-3/

Haynie, D. (2020). *Report: American quality of life declines over past decade*. US News & World Report. https://www.usnews.com/news/best-countries/articles/2020-09-11/a-global-anomaly-the-us-declines-in-annual-quality-of-life-report

Hemel, D. (2021). Can structural changes fix the Supreme Court? *The Journal of Economic Perspectives*, *35*(1), 119–142. https://www.jstor.org/stable/27008017

Herr, J. (2023, April 11). *Pros and cons of enacting Supreme Court term limits.* The Alliance for Citizen Engagement. https://ace-usa.org/blog/research/research-democratic-governance/pros-and-cons-of-enacting-supreme-court-term-limits/

History - Brown v. board of education re-enactment. (2024). United States Courts. https://www.uscourts.gov/educational-resources/educational-activities/history-brown-v-board-education-re-enactment

Houck, A. (2022, October 5). *Ketanji Brown Jackson.* Encyclopaedia Britannica. https://www.britannica.com/biography/Ketanji-Brown-Jackson

Houck, A. (2024a, October 5). *John G. Roberts, Jr.* Encyclopedia Britannica. https://www.britannica.com/biography/John-G-Roberts-Jr

Houck, A. (2024b, October 8). *Amy Coney Barrett.* Encyclopedia Britannica. https://www.britannica.com/biography/Amy-Coney-Barrett

Houk, A. M., & Smenthkowski, B. P. (2024). Samuel A. Alito, Jr. In *Encyclopædia Britannica.* https://www.britannica.com/biography/Samuel-A-Alito-Jr

Howe, A. (2023, June 29). *Supreme Court strikes down affirmative action programs in college admissions.* SCOTUSblog. https://www.scotusblog.com/2023/06/supreme-court-strikes-down-affirmative-action-programs-in-college-admissions/

Howe, A. (2024, July 26). *Court schedules first cases for 2024-25 term.* SCOTUSblog. https://www.scotusblog.com/2024/07/court-schedules-first-cases-for-2024-25-term/

Ingold, D. (2017, April 7). *Eighty is the new seventy as Supreme Court justices serve longer and longer.* Bloomberg. https://www.bloomberg.com/graphics/2017-supreme-court-justice-tenure/

Islamic Law. (n.d.). Judiciaries Worldwide. https://judiciariesworldwide.fjc.gov/islamic-law

Judicial review landmark cases. (2014). The Judicial Learning Center. https://judiciallearningcenter.org/the-power-of-judicial-review/

Judicial tenure. (n.d.). Judiciaries Worldwide. https://judiciariesworldwide.fjc.gov/judicial-tenure

Judiciaries worldwide: A resource on comparative judicial practice. (n.d.). Judiciaries Worldwide. https://judiciariesworldwide.fjc.gov/

Kaplan, J., Elliott, J., & Mierjeski, A. (2023, April 6). *Clarence Thomas secretly accepted luxury trips from major GOP donor.* ProPublica. https://www.propublica.org/article/clarence-thomas-scotus-undisclosed-luxury-travel-gifts-crow

Khanna, R. (2021, August 31). *H.R.5140 - 117th congress (2021-2022): Supreme court term limits and regular appointments act of 2021.* United States Congress. https://www.congress.gov/bill/117th-congress/house-bill/5140

Kiley, J. (2024, September 25). *Majority of Americans continue to favor moving away from electoral college.* Pew Research Center. https://www.pewresearch.org/short-reads/2024/09/25/majority-of-americans-continue-to-favor-moving-away-from-electoral-college/

Kiralfy, A. R., & Glendon, M. A. (2018). Common law. In *Encyclopædia Britannica.* https://www.britannica.com/topic/common-law

Klaidman, D., Hymes, C., & Kaplan, M. (2024, October 3). *Top justice dept. official warns of "onslaught" of foreign election interference from Russia, Iran and China.* CBS News. https://www.cbsnews.com/news/justice-department-official-warns-foreign-election-interference-russia-iran-china/

Landmark supreme court cases. (2020, January 23). Brennan Center for Justice. https://www.brennancenter.org/our-work/research-reports/landmark-supreme-court-cases

Legal Traditions. (n.d.). Judiciaries Worldwide. https://judiciariesworldwide.fjc.gov/legal-traditions

Levendusky, M., Patterson, S., Margolis, M., Pasek, J., Winneg, K., & Jamieson, K. H. (2024). Has the Supreme Court become just another political branch? Public perceptions of court approval and legitimacy in a post-*Dobbs* world. *Science Advances, 10*(10). https://doi.org/10.1126/sciadv.adk9590

Levy, M. (2019). Elena Kagan. In *Encyclopædia Britannica.* https://www.britannica.com/biography/Elena-Kagan

Life tenure for federal judges raises issues of senility, dementia. (2011, January 18). ProPublica. https://www.propublica.org/article/life-tenure-for-federal-judges-raises-issues-of-senility-dementia

Lifetime tenure for Supreme Court justices has outlived its usefulness. (2024, October 2). Brennan Center for Justice. https://www.brennancenter.org/our-work/analysis-opinion/lifetime-tenure-supreme-court-justices-has-outlived-its-usefulness

LII Collection: US Supreme Court decisions. (n.d.). Cornell Law. https://www.law.cornell.edu/supct/supremes.htm

List of nominations to the Supreme Court of the United States. (2024, July 8). Wikipedia. https://en.wikipedia.org/w/index.php?title=List_of_nominations_to_the_Supreme_Court_of_the_United_States&oldid=1233338900

Major supreme court cases from the 2023–24 term. (2024, February 8). Encyclopaedia Britannica. https://www.britannica.com/topic/major-Supreme-Court-cases-from-the-2023-24-term-2232860

Marcum, A. (2018, December 3). *Arguments against 18-year term limits for the Supreme Court.* R Street Institute. https://www.rstreet.org/research/arguments-against-18-year-term-limits-for-the-supreme-court/

MattW1105. (2022). *CMV: Supreme Court Justices should have term limits.* Reddit. https://www.reddit.com/r/changemyview/comments/t9vty4/cmv_supreme_court_justices_should_have_term_limits/

Micich, A. (2024, August 15). *How misinformation on social media has changed news.* U.S. PIRG Education Fund. https://pirg.org/edfund/articles/misinformation-on-social-media/

Moodie, D., & Siegel, H. (2022, May 3). *Ruth Bader Ginsburg could probably have saved Roe by retiring.* The Daily Beast. https://www.thedailybeast.com/ruth-bader-ginsburg-could-probably-have-saved-roe-by-retiring/

Moore v. Harper. (2023, June 27). SCOTUSblog. https://www.scotusblog.com/case-files/cases/moore-v-harper-2/

Navarro, M. (2023, April 28). *Why Supreme Court justices should have term limits and a code of ethics.* Brennan Center for Justice. https://www.brennancenter.org/our-work/analysis-opinion/why-supreme-court-justices-should-have-term-limits-and-code-ethics

Northup, N. (2018, March 19). *Supreme court case: Dobbs v. Jackson women's health organization.* Center for Reproductive Rights. https://reproductiverights.org/case/scotus-mississippi-abortion-ban/

October term 2022. (n.d.). SCOTUSblog. https://www.scotusblog.com/case-files/terms/ot2022/

Overview of Article V, amending the constitution. (n.d.). Legal Information Institute. https://www.law.cornell.edu/constitution-conan/article-5/overview-of-article-v-amending-the-constitution

Parrott-Sheffer, C. (2024). Sonia Sotomayor. In *Encyclopædia Britannica.* https://www.britannica.com/biography/Sonia-Sotomayor

Plessy v. Ferguson (1896). (2021, September 14). The U.S. National Archives and Records Administration. https://www.archives.gov/milestone-documents/plessy-v-ferguson

Proposals to modify supreme court justices' tenure: Legal considerations. (2021). In *CRS Reports.* https://crsreports.congress.gov/product/pdf/R/R46731

Pros and cons of potential term limits for Supreme Court justices. (2014, March 25). Columbia Law School. https://www.law.columbia.edu/news/archive/pros-and-cons-potential-term-limits-supreme-court-justices

Public opinion on abortion. (2024, May 13). Pew Research Center's Religion & Public Life Project. https://www.pewresearch.org/religion/fact-sheet/public-opinion-on-abortion/

Raji, T. (2024, September 13). *Poll: Americans favor Supreme Court term limits, oppose more justices.* Washington Post; The Washington Post. https://www.washingtonpost.com/politics/2024/09/13/supreme-court-term-limits-justices-poll/

Reilly, C. (2024, August 13). *Biggest lobbying interests buck trend with higher 2024 spending.* Roll Call. https://rollcall.com/2024/08/13/biggest-lobbying-interests-buck-trend-with-higher-2024-spending/

Repucci, S., & Slipowitz, A. (2022). *The global expansion of authoritarian rule.* Freedom House. https://freedomhouse.org/report/freedom-world/2022/global-expansion-authoritarian-rule

Romero, S., & Mega, E. R. (2024, September 11). Why nearly all judges in Mexico could soon be chosen by voters. *The New York Times.* https://www.nytimes.com/2024/09/11/world/americas/mexico-judiciary-overhaul.html

Saad, L. (2023, July 6). *Historically low faith in U.S. institutions continues.* Gallup. https://news.gallup.com/poll/508169/historically-low-faith-institutions-continues.aspx

Saks, A. (2022). *Quality of life decreases for the lower class; the U.S. ranks second-tier nation.* The Inkblot. https://theinkblotnews.com/12262/in-depth/quality-of-life-decreases-for-the-lower-class-the-u-s-ranks-second-tier-nation/

Schaffer, M. (2022, June 10). *"Extraordinarily self-centered": As a Roe reversal looms, RBG admirers wrestle with her legacy.* Politico. https://www.politico.com/news/magazine/2022/06/10/ruth-bader-ginsburg-retire-legacy-00038638

Schwarz, Jr., F. A. O. (2019, September 13). *Saving the Supreme Court.* Brennan Center for Justice. https://www.brennancenter.org/our-work/analysis-opinion/saving-supreme-court

Scroope, C. (2022a). *Christianity: Protestant: Laws and ethics.* Cultural Atlas. https://culturalatlas.sbs.com.au/religions/christianity-protestant/resources/christianity-protestant-law-and-ethics

Scroope, C. (2022b). *Judaism: Law and ethics.* Cultural Atlas. https://culturalatlas.sbs.com.au/religions/judaism/resources/judaism-law-and-ethics

Shapiro, I. (2021). *The politics of Supreme Court confirmations and recommendations for reform.* Cato Institute. https://www.cato.org/testimony/perspectives-supreme-court-practitioners-views-confirmation-process

Shelden, R. (2024, October 8). *A transformed Supreme Court requires different solutions.* Brennan Center for Justice. https://www.brennancenter.org/our-work/analysis-opinion/transformed-supreme-court-requires-different-solutions

Sherry, S., & Sundby, C. (2019a, April 5). *Academic highlight: The risks of Supreme Court term limits.* SCOTUSblog. https://www.scotusblog.com/2019/04/academic-highlight-the-risks-of-supreme-court-term-limits/

Sherry, S., & Sundby, C. (2019b). The risks of Supreme Court term limits. *SCOTUSblog*, https://www.scotusblog.com/2019/04/academic–highlight-the-risks-of-supreme-court-term-limits/. https://scholarship.law.vanderbilt.edu/faculty-publications/1091/

Shipan, C. R., & Shannon, M. (2003). Delaying justice(s): A duration analysis of Supreme Court confirmations. *American Journal of Political Science*, *47*(4), 654–654. https://doi.org/10.2307/3186125

Should RBG have retired in 2013? (2022). Reddit. https://www.reddit.com/r/AskFeminists/comments/usiovr/should_rbg_have_retired_in_2013/

Smentkowski, B. (2019). Supreme Court of the United States. In *Encyclopædia Britannica*. https://www.britannica.com/topic/Supreme-Court-of-the-United-States

Smentkowski, B. P. (2019). Clarence Thomas. In *Encyclopædia Britannica*. https://www.britannica.com/biography/Clarence-Thomas

Smentkowski, B., & Houck, A. (2019). Brett Kavanaugh. In *Encyclopædia Britannica*. https://www.britannica.com/biography/Brett-Kavanaugh

Smith, J. F. (2020, July 13). *U.S. Supreme Court v. American public opinion: The verdict is in*. Harvard Kennedy School of Law. https://www.hks.harvard.edu/faculty-research/policy-topics/democracy-governance/us-supreme-court-v-american-public-opinion

Sonia Sotomayor. (n.d.). National Museum of the American Latino. https://latino.si.edu/exhibitions/presente/shaping-nation/sonia-sotomayor

Sprunt, B. (2020, October 26). *Amy Coney Barrett confirmed to supreme court, takes constitutional oath*. NPR. https://www.npr.org/2020/10/26/927640619/senate-confirms-amy-coney-barrett-to-the-supreme-court

Stening, T. (2024, May 29). *Supreme Court's 2024 term is coming to a close. Here are five big decisions expected within just days.* Northeastern Global News. https://news.northeastern.edu/2024/05/29/upcoming-supreme-court-cases-2024-term/

Students for fair admissions inc. v. president & fellows of Harvard college. (n.d.). SCOTUSblog. https://www.scotusblog.com/case-files/cases/students-for-fair-admissions-inc-v-president-fellows-of-harvard-college/

Supreme court and congress. (2020). Library of Congress. https://constitution.congress.gov/browse/essay/artIII-S1-8-3/ALDE_00013559/

The Supreme Court of the United States - history. (n.d.). United States Senate Committee on the Judiciary. https://www.judiciary.senate.gov/nominations/supreme-court/history/

The Supreme Court has been expanded many times before. Here are four ways to do it today. (2019, May 6). Harvard Law & Policy Review. https://journals.law.harvard.edu/lpr/2019/05/06/the-supreme-court-has-been-expanded-many-times-before-here-are-four-ways-to-do-it-today/

Supreme Court seen as out of touch. (2022, September 30). Monmouth University Polling Institute. https://www.monmouth.edu/polling-institute/reports/monmouthpoll_us_093022/

Supreme court term limits. (2023). In American Academy of Arts and Sciences. https://www.amacad.org/sites/default/files/publication/downloads/2023_SCOTUS-Term-Limits.pdf

Supreme court term october 2022: A review of selected major rulings. (2023). In Congressional Research Service. https://crsreports.congress.gov/product/pdf/R/R47689

Taylor, III, W. W. (2023, January 25). *How the Supreme Court is destroying its own legitimacy.* Alliance for Justice. https://afj.org/article/how-the-supreme-court-is-destroying-its-own-legitimacy/

10 fascinating facts about the Supreme Court on its birthday. (n.d.). National Constitution Center. https://constitutioncenter.org/blog/10-fascinating-facts-on-the-supreme-courts-birthday

303 Creative LLC v. Elenis. (2023, June 30). SCOTUSblog. https://www.scotusblog.com/case-files/cases/303-creative-llc-v-elenis/

Topic: Supreme Court. (n.d.). Roper iPoll: Cornell University Roper Center for Public Opinion Research. https://ropercenter.cornell.edu/ipoll/search?q=Supreme+Court

Traister, R. (2020, September 19). *It shouldn't have come down to her.* The Cut. https://www.thecut.com/2020/09/ruth-bader-ginsburg-anger.html

Transitional justice. (n.d.). Judiciaries Worldwide. https://judiciariesworldwide.fjc.gov/transitional-justice

Twenty-seventh amendment. (2024). In *Encyclopædia Britannica.* https://www.britannica.com/topic/Twenty-seventh-Amendment

Two centuries later: The enduring legacy of Marbury v. Madison (1803). (2005, March). United States Courts. https://www.uscourts.gov/sites/default/files/judicial-review_0.pdf

U.S. Constitution - article III. (1787). US Congress. https://constitution.congress.gov/constitution/article-3/

U.S. Election Assistance Commission. (2011). *The electoral college.* https://www.govinfo.gov/content/pkg/GOVPUB-Y3_EL2_5-PURL-gpo77477/pdf/GOVPUB-Y3_EL2_5-PURL-gpo77477.pdf

van Dijk, F. (2020). Judiciary in democracy: Alignment and disconnect. *Springer EBooks*, 93–109. https://doi.org/10.1007/978-3-030-63143-7_7

Walsh, D. (2020, October 15). *Takeaways from Amy Coney Barrett's judiciary confirmation hearings.* NPR. https://www.npr.org/2020/10/15/923637375/takeaways-from-amy-coney-barretts-judiciary-confirmation-hearings

Washington, G. (2024, September 23). *A changing supreme court: Politics and polarization - A conversation with political science professor Brandon Bartels.* The George Washington University Columbian College of Arts & Sciences. https://vimeo.com/658779920

What should we expect from Biden's commission on Supreme Court reform? (n.d.). Brookings. https://www.brookings.edu/articles/what-should-we-expect-from-bidens-commission-on-supreme-court-reform/

What Supreme Court justices said about Roe and abortion in their confirmations. (2022, June 24). NBC News. https://www.nbcnews.com/politics/supreme-court/supreme-court-justices-said-roe-abortion-confirmations-rcna35246

Wheeler, R. (2020, March 2). *Should we restructure the Supreme Court?* Brookings. https://www.brookings.edu/articles/should-we-restructure-the-supreme-court/

Wood, D. (2024). *Why term limits for Supreme Court justices make sense.* Brennan Center for Justice. https://www.brennancenter.org/our-work/analysis-opinion/why-term-limits-supreme-court-justices-make-sense

Zeitz, J. (2022, April 3). *The Supreme Court has never been apolitical.* Politico. https://www.politico.com/news/magazine/2022/04/03/the-supreme-court-has-never-been-apolitical-00022482

Made in the USA
Monee, IL
04 November 2026

67384091R00089